Archaeology from The Ploughsoil

Studies in the Collection and Interpretation of Field Survey data

Edited by

Colin Haselgrove, Martin Millett and Ian Smith

D1579737

Department of Archaeology and Prehistory
University of Sheffield

© Individual Authors, 1985
Publisher: John R. Collis
Editor: Val Kinsler
Cover: Chris Unwin
Typist: Jacinta Edmonds

British Library Cataloguing in Publication Data
    Archaeology from the ploughsoil: studies in the collection
    and interpretation of field survey data.
1.   Archaeological surveying
I. Haselgrove, Colin   II. Millett, Martin   III. Smith, Ian
930.1'028   CC76.3

ISBN 0-906090-24-5

Department of Archaeology and Prehistory
University of Sheffield
Sheffield S10 2TN

Printed by H. Charlesworth & Co. Ltd.,
Huddersfield, England.

Contents

List of Figures

List of Tables

List of Contributors

Edward Cloutman — *Department of Plant Sciences, University College, Cardiff.*

David Crowther — *Hull City Museums, Town Docks Museum, Queen Victoria Square, Kingston-upon-Hull.*

Charles French — *Fenland Archaeological Associates, Sycamore Farm House, Seadyke Bank, Wisbech St. Mary, Cambridgeshire.*

Charles Gaffney — *School of Archaeological Sciences, University of Bradford.*

Vince Gaffney — *81 High Trees Close, Redditch, Hereford and Worcester.*

Colin Haselgrove — *Department of Archaeology, University of Durham.*

Robin Holgate — *Archaeological Field Unit, Institute of Archaeology, London.*

Martin Millett — *Department of Archaeology, University of Durham.*

Nigel Mills — *Department of Archaeology and Prehistory, University of Sheffield.*

Francis Pryor — *Fenland Archaeological Associates, Sycamore Farm House, Seadyke Bank, Wisbech St. Mary, Cambridgeshire.*

Tim Schadla-Hall — *Leicestershire Museums, 96 New Walk, Leicester*

Ian Smith — *Royal Commission on Ancient and Historical Monuments(Scotland), Edinburgh.*

Martin Tingle — *9 Eastern Avenue, Reading.*

Lucy Walker — *13 Nevilledale Terrace, Durham.*

Introduction

Not a Universal Panacea, but ...

The papers that constitute the core of this volume were originally solicited in connection with a poster-session at the fourth annual conference of the Theoretical Archaeology Group which took place at Durham in December 1982. This display and the connected discussion was organised by John Bintliff and Ian Smith. The interest expressed in the papers and the ideas they generated in an unusually interesting and frank exchange of views led the present editors to invite the original contributors and others to commit ideas and experience to print as a more formal statement of some of the views expressed on that occasion.

The decision to organise a poster-session on theory and method in field survey design was in itself a reflection of the dramatic expansion in this sphere of archaeology on both sides of the Atlantic over the past twenty years and the innovations in technique which this has stimulated. Historically, this phenomenon had its roots in the accelerating impact of modern development on the archaeological record and the general consciousness-raising which is now among the most tangible legacies of the Cultural Resources and Rescue movements. There, admittedly, the similarity ends. For a long time developments on either Continent were along markedly divergent paths which owed as much to differences in the nature of the archaeological record as to the intellectual traditions which these had fostered. Thus in a Europe shocked and profoundly depressed by the realisation that far from already knowing the essentials of its rich and varied cultural heritage, it was all still to do, despite the centuries of interest and collection of information about the past, many surveys took the form of infinitessimally detailed studies of relatively small areas—the Parish, or the line of a motorway for instance. Overall, the tenor of thought was decidedly negative—'very well, if it is a case of having to begin all over again anyway, we might as well start by doing a survey ...'

In the United States, the situation was very different from the start. New developments were frequently affecting areas which had never previously received formal archaeological investigation and about which next to nothing was known. As a result, survey—which was usually employed in an expansive role and in *de novo* archaeological investigations—rapidly became caught up in the wave of optimism which was sweeping American Archaeology as the chosen instrument of that movement; the role in fact (harnessed to probabilistic sampling theory) in which it had prophetically been cast by Binford in May 1963 in his seminal consideration of archaeological research design (Binford, 1964). The past was 'knowable' in all essentials, the only question—apart from some 'minor' theoretical and methodological problems which still had to be solved—was how soon.

Partly because of the different worlds into which systematic survey was born, partly as a result of the combination of suspicion and downright hostility with which this New American dream was greeted by the vast majority of European archaeologists, it was not until the late 1970s that the genuine methodological advances achieved in the New World began to have an obvious impact on the theory and practice of survey in Britain and Europe. Its eventual arrival was marked by the meetings which gave rise to such important volumes as those edited by Cherry *et al.* (1978) and Hinchliffe and Schadla-Hall (1980). Even at that stage, however, the 'reformation' was far from complete, with the editors of the former volume finding themselves constrained to admit that their views on sampling and thus, by implication, on the overall aims and design of survey, were diametrically opposed to those of many of their contributors (Cherry *et al.,* 1978: xiv).

Nevertheless, it is clear in retrospect that this period was the crucial turning point in the attitude of many British and European archaeologists to survey and its importance for the study of past populations. This has been evident in the multiplication of rigorous survey work which has taken place since that date. Our impression, however, and one of the major reasons behind the present volume, is that neither the quality of the objectives nor the interpretative frameworks applied have been evolving at anything like the rate necessary to match the sheer explosion in the quantity of data generated in this upsurge of interest. Despite the pioneering volumes which have already been mentioned, and a number of isolated exceptions (e.g. Crowther, 1983), many surveys still seem to have as their primary objective the addition of more or less undifferentiated dots to a distribution map, whether they are ultimately intended to adorn the academic bookshop or more pragmatically, the planner's office. Not unsurprisingly, such seemingly blinkered aims are causing not a few leading archaeologists to continue to question the allocation of even the very minimal resources that survey requires (see Fowler, 1980).

While sympathising with such views to a point, our feeling is very much the opposite: that the full potential of survey and its most obvious concomitants, topsoil assemblages and so-called 'ploughsoil archaeology' have yet to be widely recognised, let alone properly explored; a question of having only 'scratched the surface' if ever there was one.

Much of this, of course, results from the common view that ploughsoil material is unstratified, the end product of the plough destroying stratification beneath, which has led to a concentration on plough damage surveys and more seriously to the assumption, implicit in many excavation research designs, that the topsoil can be machined away without any significant information loss. This assumption not only ignores the information potential of the topsoil, but is more sinister because it allows those designing public policy to put aside not only the problems of agricultural damage, serious though these undoubtedly are in many areas, on the grounds that *all* areas suffer, but also the claim that more detailed study of the topsoil would be worthwhile. The editors of this volume feel that the evidence now available, including that from several of the papers published here demand a reassessment of this attitude since topsoil can be shown to be a valuable archaeological resource in its own right.

The papers in Part 1 of this volume are concerned with the development of the methodology which we believe is required if the promise of survey is ever to be fulfilled in this respect. The main thrust of the section is the establishment of theoretical frameworks explaining the relationship between subsoil and topsoil archaeology, the processes governing the formation of topsoil assemblages, and the principles to be applied in extracting meaning from them. Only with these, will elucidation of the connections between distribution patterns and past human activities become possible. These methodological themes are taken up in Part 2, which is designed to present not so much a review of results as a series of studies which explore, in practice, the problems of which we are aware in theory. These case studies are organised according to the scale at which the problems are examined, from the region down to the landscape unit. A particular problem explored in Chapters 5 and 6 is that of the buried landscape. In the Fenland example, the practical and theoretical problems of undertaking such a landscape study are explored in detail whilst the Vale of Pickering is used to demonstrate the potential of an approach based on palaeogeographical survey. Both papers provide examples of the problems which face all those concerned with survey on a less dramatic scale. The final papers, dealing with small scale, but detailed, work raise important issues about the meaning of topsoil assemblages in relation to conventionally defined sites. The Maddle Farm project, in particular, seems to point the way to a new era in our understanding of the detail of past landscapes.

Our aim in presenting the papers has been to be selective, and to address what appear to be key problems. We have not tried to be comprehensive, and have deliberately omitted papers on related themes (e.g. aerial photography). We have also avoided trying to produce a textbook, while hoping that the contents provide some bridge between theory and practice. We are concerned that survey should not appear as a universal panacea, but equally that it should not be dismissed for failing to provide all the answers. Those who support either extreme should reflect on the late John Morris'

> "elephant trap which still tempts the unwary archaeologist, the overconfident notion that what he cannot recognise does not exist" (1975: 343)

To be used properly we believe that survey should not remain an end in itself but must be integrated into archaeological research designs such that survey, excavation, finds analysis and social reconstruction are parts of a single coherent and consistent whole. If this approach is followed, then our understanding of past settlement patterns and landscapes can only be enhanced—this certainly is the collective message of the papers presented here.

Acknowledgements

We are extremely grateful to all those who assisted in the production of the volume, particularly Yvonne Brown, Tom Middlemass and Trevor Woods for their assistance in the preparation of the figures, Val Kinsler for her editorial work and Tina Hartas and Sheila Sutherland for the translation of the abstracts.

Bibliography

Binford, L.R. 1964 A consideration of archaeological research design. *American Antiquity* 29: 425–441

Cherry, J., Gamble, C. and Shennan, S. 1978 *Sampling in Contemporary British Archaeology*. Oxford: British Archaeological Reports British Series 50

Crowther, D.R. 1983 Old land surfaces and modern ploughsoil. *Scottish Archaeological Review* 2: 31–44

Fowler, P.J. 1980 Tradition and objectives in British archaeology 1953–1978. *Archaeological Journal* 137: 1–21

Hinchliffe, J. and Schadla-Hall, R.T. (eds.) 1980 *The Past under the Plough*. London: DOE (Occasional Paper 3)

Morris, J. 1975 London's decline AD 150–250. *London Archaeologist* 2: 343–4

PART 1

METHODOLOGICAL PROBLEMS

1. Inference from Ploughsoil Artefact Samples

by Colin Haselgrove

In recent years, the deliberate collection of unstratified ploughsoil finds has taken on greater prominence in archaeological fieldwork, not surprisingly, since the techniques involved are both cheap and simple, and, at a basic level at least, appear to be very effective. In most areas where systematic ground surveys have taken place, dozens, often literally hundreds, of new sites have been recorded, many of them virtually impossible to detect by any other technique (Holgate, this volume). Fieldwalking also seems to offer a means of documenting some of the many human activities which took place beyond the confines of the domestic habitation (Gaffney *et al.,* this volume). In general, it is now recognised as an essential component of any investigation of regional settlement patterns and land-use (Mills, this volume). In addition, where sites are initially suggested by other kinds of evidence, notably cropmarks, systematic collection of artefacts over disturbed areas often yields information invaluable to their classification and dating (e.g. Foard, 1978; Woodward, 1978). When a site is excavated, preliminary surface survey can be helpful in identifying patterning within the site, while topsoil screening as part of the excavation process has often yielded many of the most significant artefact finds (*cf.* Gingell, 1980) and may be especially informative where the site belongs to a cultural horizon lacking much by way of durable artefacts or when the topsoil features are predominantly structural.

Unstratified surface material is thus already important in archaeological thinking, and, moreover, is likely to become increasingly so, as the gulf between the number of sites excavated and those known, but destined to remain unexcavated, steadily widens. For the latter, it will often be the only kind of evidence available to establish their character and context. In the circumstances, one would expect the interpretation and potential of ploughsoil artefact samples to be matters of vigorous debate. As it is, with a few notable exceptions (e.g. Crowther, 1983; Foley, 1981) most archaeologists clearly do not consider the matter to merit serious concern and are content to accept a great deal of fieldwork data at its face value.

In my view, this complacency is ill-founded, and apparent in a number of serious misconceptions embedded in the literature. It is the purpose of this paper to draw attention to some of those, and, in doing so, to suggest that there is a great deal which could be done to improve the situation. It will be argued that what is lacking, in effect, is a methodology tailored to the very specific problems of unstratified ploughsoil material and its interpretation. Only by doing this, can the deficiencies inherent in this kind of evidence be recognised—whether they relate to cultural factors or to archaeological method—and the means of compensating for them be devised, while on the positive side, only when we think through what information ought to be latent in unstratified material, can we come up with suitable methods for extracting it. In this regard, underwater archaeology is significantly in advance of its terrestrial counterpart. Maritime archaeologists accept that in order to recover the original associations or patterning of artefacts on a sunken vessel, a series of "filters" have first to be applied to the wrecking event and subsequent scrambling processes, and an explicit methodology has therefore been proposed, together with a number of techniques which have been tested for their potential in extracting information from sea-bed distributions (Muckelroy, 1978).

The analogy between "post-depositional" scrambling processes underwater, and the complex and (for friable artefacts) destructive cycles of displacement, exposure and weathering, and reburial, experienced by artefacts in a cultivated horizon is a particularly close one and would repay further attention. There can be no dispute that the additional sorting processes which ploughsoil assemblages have undergone compared to most other buried material adds significantly to the difficulty of their interpretation, and as such must be the subject of further study. In this respect, it is unfortunate that although ploughing has received a great deal of attention from archaeologists in recent years (e.g. Hinchliffe and Schadla-Hall, 1980; Lambrick, 1977), the focus has been predominantly on its destructive agency, rather than its effects on artefacts which have already been incorporated. Even so, a number of significant conclusions have been reached, undeniably the most important being that on relatively flat surfaces, there is usually little significant lateral displacement (Gingell, 1980), and thus that the original spatial structure of artefact distributions should be recoverable. Displacement is only a problem on slopes where there is significant soil-creep.

No inference is better than its inherent assumptions or the coherence of its constituent arguments, and for those to be made explicit will only strengthen interpretation. Indeed, critical scrutiny of these is essential if field walking and surface collection results are to have any value beyond the most mundane level of observation and prediction. At present, many of the claims advanced for such results must be ranked as more or less speculation, but if even a few of them could be demonstrated to have a reasonable chance of validity, this would have profound implications for the balance that we could then afford to maintain between fieldwork and excavation. This could only be welcome in view of the very limited resources currently available to archaeology. It is as a contribution to this task, using examples mainly drawn from recent survey work in the Aisne Valley, France (Haselgrove, 1983) that the following discussion is offered. For reasons which will be readily apparent, its emphasis will be on the status and interpretation of those clusters of surface finds which find their way into the literature or SMRs as "sites", sometimes with precariously little justification.

Ploughsoil Artefact Samples: Definition and Status

Many misconceptions surrounding the interpretation of fieldwalking results have arisen as a result of simple failure to clarify the nature of the relevant material and its potential relationship to other aspects of the archaeological record. Fieldwork data comes in many forms, for instance artefacts exposed on uncultivated surfaces through weathering, but here we are concerned with one aspect only: the procedures invoked in making inferences from a particular kind of *sample* of artefacts drawn from a particular *context*; cultivated soil horizons. In other words, material recovered, by whatever means, from definite albeit unreachable, *target populations: all* the artefacts in ploughsoils in a given region which, for a rural region like Wessex, can be a dense and near continuous distribution of artefacts across the landscape (*cf.* Schadla-Hall and Shennan, 1978). In practice, however, it is convenient to exclude previously cultivated land now under pasture from this conceptual target population (since material is only likely to be recovered through the excavation of underlying deposits). Equally, in some areas like north-east England, certain modern cultivation soils must be discounted as "zones of destruction"; for example where ploughsoil has been reconstituted after open-cast mining and cannot possibly retain any significant degree of artefact patterning relating to earlier periods. In any area, the proportions of the land-surface currently under cultivation will clearly be a major determinant of what kind of inferences on a regional (as opposed to a site-specific) scale are likely to be permissible—a point which should be obvious, but which all too frequently appears to have been overlooked in the design of survey programmes. A significant factor in the decision to invest resources in a regional fieldwalking programme in the Aisne Valley was that approximately 80% of the study area is under intensive cultivation, rising to over 90% on the Champagne chalklands.

For this reason alone, it is necessary to expose an important distinction, one which is unfortunately all too often collapsed in practice, between the *sampled population* and the *target population*, the former being the proportion of the latter which is actually *available* for investigation. In terms of the geographical extent of cultivated areas, the two are often synonymous providing the individual fields chosen for sampling are all accessible. However, in other crucial respects, they clearly are not the same. Only a tiny proportion of the artefacts is actually exposed and visible on the surface, and thus collectable, at any one time—often as little as 2% Crowther (1983) suggests in the case of Maxey. Moreover, the cycle of exposure and burial which artefacts in the ploughsoil undergo, ensures that the surface (and therefore the sampled) population is constantly undergoing renewal. Theoretically, at least, an identical collection exercise on two separate occasions could give us totally contrasting results.

On the other hand, I see no conceptual basis for differentiating between ploughsoil artefact samples according to their mode of collection; *all* are samples. In each case, however, the sampled population differs. So therefore does the relationship between sample and the ultimate target population, which in turn conditions what inferences may legitimately be drawn. Thus for fieldwalking the sampled population consists of those artefacts currently visible on the surface, a minimal percentage of the overall ploughsoil assemblage, whereas an excavated sample, or one obtained by careful screening of the topsoil, *ought* to represent the bulk of the finds to be made in that particular area. Metal detector finds constitute another kind of sample, albeit a very skewed one, carrying with them a number of uncertainties arising out of the type of equipment used and the manner of its operation (Crowther, 1981). However, with a penetration which is usually shallow in relation to the average depth of ploughsoil, the risk of "contamination" by material dislodged from undisturbed subsoil deposits is probably low.

It is supposedly in the nature of the threat posed by contemporary agricultural practices that the available target populations are never static in their composition. New artefacts, we are led to believe (Hinchliffe and Schadla-Hall, 1980), are constantly being liberated into cultivated soil horizons as underlying archaeological deposits are disturbed, while the less durable elements of the existing assemblage are abraded and broken down by plough action or physical weathering, although there is, in fact, remarkably little information available from which to gauge the seriousness of these problems. The results of experiments specifically designed to monitor these processes (Reynolds and Schadla-Hall, 1980) will be a fundamental contribution in this area of study.

Most important of all, however, is that surface artefact collections cease to be invested with a mythical status as all sorts of things they patently are not. Despite a number of warnings to the contrary (Foley, 1981), clusters of artefacts continue to be converted unthinkingly into "sites", yet even when it can be established that a concentration represents a genuine departure from background distributional trends, the resultant construct is of very dubious interpretative value. Many factors can generate apparent clustering, often completely unrelated to the past activities which interest us. The other common misconception to be found in the literature is that there is necessarily a relationship between material in ploughsoil, and that in underlying deposits or earthbound features, something which is most certainly *not* the case; this is largely responsible for an attitude which has seen surface collection dismissed as a pursuit markedly inferior to excavation, a distorted reflection of the underlying reality, when, in fact, these generally deal with different and potentially complementary forms of evidence.

If interpretation is not to be wholly erroneous, samples of unstratified ploughsoil assemblages must be treated for what they are: as an unknown, their composition (as with the contents of any other archaeological deposit) a matter for explanation in terms of *all* the processes which contributed to their formation; their relationship to any other archaeological features as something for investigation rather than assumption. In this way, spurious patterns with little or nothing to do with the behaviour which concerns us can be readily eliminated, leaving the remainder as a much more certain basis for our studies of a particular area, culture or region.

A Model for Inference from Ploughsoil Artefact Samples (Fig. 1.1)

A number of distinct conceptual stages, then, are involved when inferences are drawn from collections of artefacts obtained by fieldwalking or surface collection; these have been set out formally in Figure 1.1. It is obvious that at a methodological level there is a basic dichotomy between the process of arguing from a sample back to the artefact population from which it was drawn, and that of using that sample as a basis to make statements about the patterns of past human behaviour. For the one, the only factors which intervene between us and the population under investigation are essentially controllable, e.g. the collection techniques utilized or the recovery rate achieved. One hundred per cent recovery (such that the sample *is* the sampled population) is perfectly plausible, if only rarely practicable and potentially wasteful. For the latter, there is inevitably an enormous gap between the material culture which has survived and that which was originally in use, to say nothing of the difficulties of deciding what activities are represented by any patterns of discard or loss we have succeeded in identifying. The cultural and natural processes which formed the archaeological record as we find it today, as such, are completely outside our control, and the best we can do is to make allowances for their operation. Giving meaning to any of our observations, therefore calls for a complex set of arguments, assumptions and generalisations, some of them specifically archaeological, others originally developed in a different context such as geology but obviously of relevance. To designate this whole series of interpretative operations and principles the realm of *archaeological inference*, as do e.g. Cherry *et al.,* (1978), seems perfectly appropriate.

As we have seen, intervening between these two major concerns, there is generally a third implied by the distinction between sampled population and target population. While these may be more or less identical—for example, when the ploughsoil covering an entire site is excavated by hand, in which case the difference is of

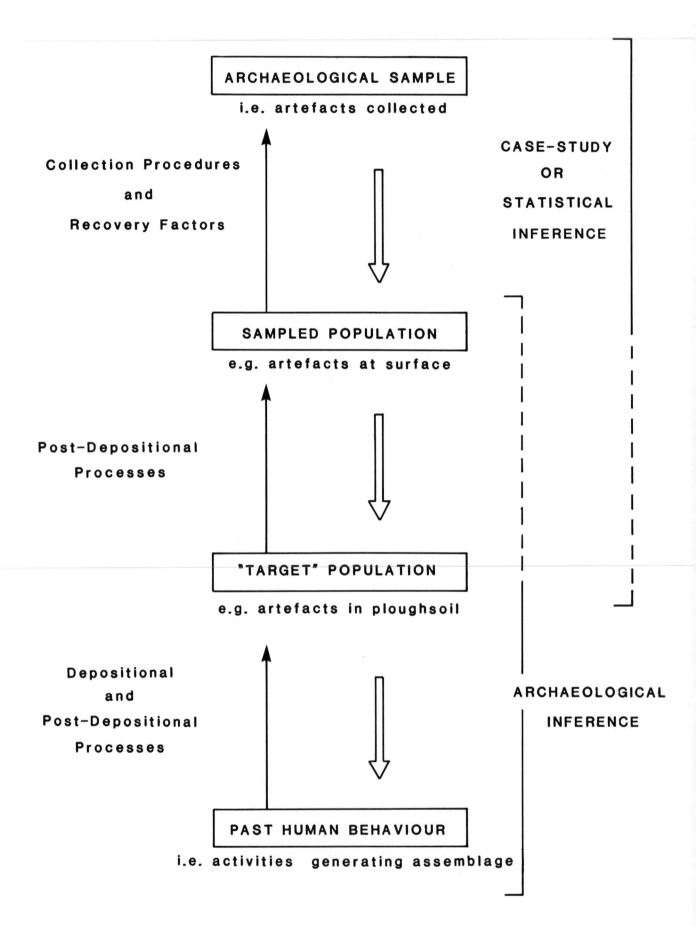

ARCHAEOLOGICAL SAMPLE

i.e. artefacts collected

Collection Procedures
and
Recovery Factors

CASE-STUDY
OR
STATISTICAL
INFERENCE

SAMPLED POPULATION

e.g. artefacts at surface

Post-Depositional
Processes

"TARGET" POPULATION

e.g. artefacts in ploughsoil

Depositional
and
Post-Depositional
Processes

ARCHAEOLOGICAL
INFERENCE

PAST HUMAN BEHAVIOUR

i.e. activities generating assemblage

Figure 1.1   A model for inference from ploughsoil assemblages.

negligible importance—more often than not the two are at a significant remove from one another. At present, an assessment of the relationship between the two must be considered as primarily within the realm of archaeological inference, since there has been so little investigation of the dynamics of ploughsoil artefact populations. In the longer-term, however, since the target population is both definite and can be recovered directly, at least in parts, and the processes which affect it can be observed and are reasonably uniform, judicious experimentation and the use of control samples (e.g. the excavation of selected units to monitor the relationship of artefacts on the surface to those concealed in the soil), should allow the principles of sample—sampled population inference to be extended in many cases to the whole of the ploughsoil assemblage.

The status of any statement about a parent population is necessarily dependent on the sampling techniques which have been employed to acquire our primary information. Thus, where probabilistic selection is a feature of a survey design, the power of statistical inference may be invoked in making generalisations about the overall character of a population. When such methods are appropriate to archaeological data is still hotly debated (Cherry *et al.*, 1978; Doran and Hodson, 1975), and doubtless such disputes will continue. One potential application, as suggested above, is in monitoring the efficiency of systematic surface collections. For many projects, whether concerned with an individual site or with a region, another must be the investigation of at least a proportion of its constituent parts chosen at random, because otherwise there will always be a danger of simply perpetuating our preconceptions or the erroneous results of earlier work.

Equally, there are many situations where a statistical sampling strategy is inadmissable, or unnecessary. The virtue of fieldwalking is that large areas can be surveyed relatively quickly, and for many problems, e.g. identifying artefact clusters and recording their extent, continuous coverage of the delimited zone will often be the most appropriate strategy. Again, with individual sites, collection over their entire surface is often perfectly feasible, and offers the best hope of bringing out any patterns on the plough soil artefact distribution. In those instances, which are known as *case-study* situations (*cf.* Doran and Hodson, 1975), the aim of the exercise is a sample representative of whatever population from which it was drawn. Inferences are dependent on the assumption that this has been achieved.

It is here, of course, that the real strength of statistical inference lies, in operating within established confidence levels (Cherry *et al.*, 1978), whereas with a case-study inference, the only arbiter is our own judgement of the probable *relationship* between a sample and its parent population. Unfortunately, owing to the polemical nature of much of the discussion which has surrounded the "sampling question", this essential point has been all but lost.

It is clearly important to ensure that assessment of this relationship is not complicated still further by the effects of over-producing factors such as differential visibility or variable recovery. By distorting our results, these have the power to alter our perception of the past and our aim must be their elimination wherever possible, or if this is impracticable, to control them and compensate for any bias which has been introduced. At this level, the difficulties of working with ploughsoil artefact samples are much the same as with many other categories of archaeological data, and although much of what has recently been written about the problems of site visibility and recovery has related to regional survey design (*cf.* various papers in Cherry *et al.*, 1978), it is applicable on the whole to survey work on any scale.

One problem concerning potential fieldwork bias which has yet to receive adequate attention is whether differences in ability or performance between one individual and another is likely to have any marked effect on the recovery of primary evidence. Unfortunately, although Clarke (1979) has shown that individual recovery rates do affect results on an excavated site, the danger seems to leave most archaeologists relatively unperturbed. Yet of all the branches of the discipline, it is fieldwork which again and again rests on the work of one or two individuals, each covering a particular area, and any consistent differences in their pattern of recovery could easily serve to prejudice the results. At Wollaston, it was noted that one experienced fieldwalker picked up a much higher percentage of sherds in the 1.5–3.5 cm. size range than did the other (Foard, 1980). As this was the range in which pagan/middle Saxon pottery is concentrated, a misleading picture of the distribution of settlement could easily have emerged. Another example is given below, and further investigation of this whole question is clearly warranted.

So too is careful consideration of the sampling intensity needed to satisfy the requirements of statistical or case-study inference. One of the most persistent delusions of the archaeological literature is that this is represented by a particular pre-conceived *sampling fraction*, usually ten per cent. In fact, what is virtually all-important is the absolute *sample size* (Cowgill, 1975). Moreover, fieldwork is an indirect sampling technique, effectively a form of cluster sampling (Cherry *et al.*, 1978), in that the areas investigated merely contain the items of interest. This complicates the situation since the density of artefacts in each collection unit is a completely independent quantity which can only be ascertained by prior investigation. For the purposes of fieldwork, it would therefore seem best to restrict the use of the term *sampling fraction* to the proportion of an area which is actually investigated, and the *sample size* to the number of artefacts actually recovered. It follows that a record of those is a pre-requisite for any meaningful analysis of the results. Thus in the case of the Aisne

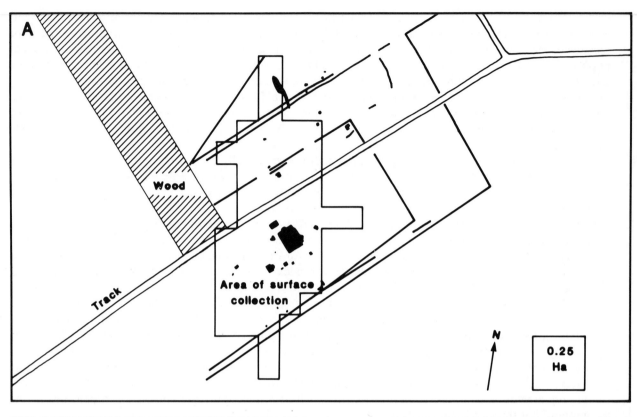

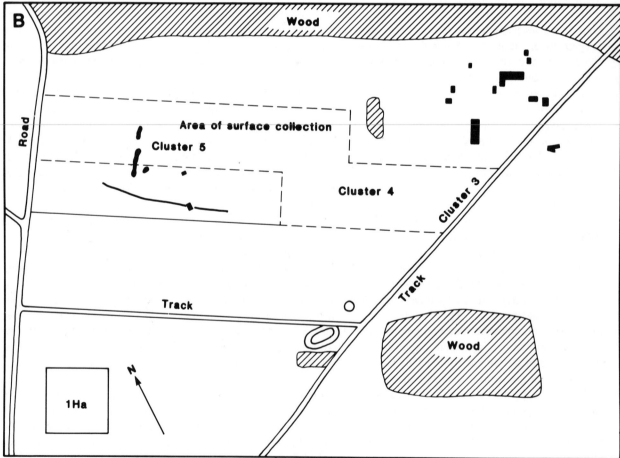

Figure 1.2 Cropmark and surface collection units at Beaurieux, Les Grèves (*BLG*) and Limé, Les Terres Noires (*LTN*).

Valley, surface collection took place over an area of 2 ha. at Beaurieux, Les Grèves (Fig. 1.2A: *BLG*) subdivided into ten metre squares, within which five transects each one metre wide were actually walked. The overall sampling fraction was thus fifty per cent and it is intended to maintain this when the remaining 2 ha. of the site are investigated. By contrast, at the much larger site of Limé, Les Terres Noires (Fig. 1.2B: *LTN*) a preliminary survey took the form of a transect 100 m. wide across the site, within which five lines two metres wide were walked. The sampling portion there was thus only ten per cent and the area investigated there represents a mere four per cent of this 20 ha. complex, in contrast to the sample from *BLG* which derives from a full quarter of the site.

The total number of iron age and Roman sherds (excluding amphora) recovered from *BLG* was 823, and from *LTN*, 1335, of which 24 and 146 respectively were in *terra sigillata* or Argonne fabrics. While it is already clear from these figures that *LTN* was the more prolific, the actual sherd densities are $0.08/m^2$ and $0.17/m^2$ (for all fabrics) and $0.0024/m^2$ and $0.02/m^2$ (for *terra sigillata* and Argonne wares). Thus at *LTN*, the overall density was greater by a factor of two and ten respectively, a discrepancy which would be greater still if the figures were calculated independently for the three major concentrations which were detected by this preliminary investigation (Fig. 1.2B). Both sites appear to be occupied over the same general period, and even without the aid of the cropmarks, it would be difficult not to conclude that we are dealing with different kinds of site. One of them (*BLG*) is in fact, a native farm which gradually becomes Romanised; the other has all the attributes of the massive Roman building complexes which are a feature of Belgic Gaul (*cf*. Haselgrove, 1983).

A major problem confronting archaeologists is to determine the adequacy of a particular size of sample as a basis for quantitative inferences about a given parent population, e.g. the relative proportion of different fabrics present in the ceramic assemblage. Whether a particular sample size will be sufficient is effectively dependent on the nature and variability of the population of interest (and where a statistical design has been used, on the precision of the estimates required). Thus, to decide what threshold is appropriate requires prior knowledge of the population (something which the archaeologist cannot reasonably be expected to possess if the purpose of the fieldwork is to establish those population characteristics) or a good guess. This is in fact, one facet of what is commonly referred to as the *sampling paradox* (Cherry *et al.*, 1978).

A common aid to the solution of this paradox, which could well be appropriate in a site-specific situation, is the use of pilot samples as a first step, before embarking on a systematic programme of surface collection. The *LTN* survey, previously mentioned, would be an example of this approach. The total surface sherd population can be estimated at c. 34,000, and depending on the variability of the fabric types present in the sample which has been collected so far, further surface collection with an appropriate sampling fraction could be carried out. The difficulty with this approach is that each site must be assessed separately.

The alternative approach, which is, in any case, normal in a case-study situation (i.e. where mathematical links between the sample and the parent population cannot be established) is probably the more useful in an archaeological context. This is to treat the sample as a meaningful population in its own right, for which various descriptive statistics can be calculated, e.g. relative frequencies, and then compared with those computed for the assemblage from another site or situation. At the most basic level, all that is involved is an assessment of the degree of similarity between two assemblages, and there are even various statistical tables which can give a useful, albeit informal, indication of the degree of confidence which can be placed in descriptive statistics computed for a given sample size (Doran and Hodson, 1975). Difficulties, however, arise when the sample is made to "stand" for the site and what must then be an *archaeological inference* is invoked to account for similarities (or differences) between the two assemblages, e.g. as indicating that the sites were occupied during the same period. The validity of the comparative exercise then hinges absolutely on each of the samples being sufficiently representative of its site, to allow such an interpretation.

We are thus once again brought back to the question of an adequate sample size—in this case, to try to ensure that samples are reasonably representative of their parent site assemblage. Experimentation under controlled conditions is clearly required for different kinds of populations, e.g. lithic assemblages or pottery groups, and with material from excavated sites of different types and period, ranging from hunter/gatherer kill sites to early medieval settlements. In each case, i.e. whatever the issue (e.g. the range of functional types in a mesolithic tool kit, or the relative proportions of different amphora fabrics present) the problem is always the same—to calculate the sample size needed to give a reasonable estimate of the variability of the parent assemblage. Such a task may sound daunting, but it needs to be undertaken if we are ever to rely on most of the inferences drawn from regional survey and surface collection programmes. It would also ensure that time and effort are not wasted in gathering information which is entirely surplus to the questions being asked.

The possibilities of such work are shown by Millett's investigation of the sample sizes needed to gauge the relative frequencies of different *terra sigillata* fabrics on a given site (Millett, 1983). He suggests that 30 identifiable vessels will prove adequate for many purposes, and criticises Hodder (1974) for relying on too meagre a sample size in his well-known study of the marketing of Savernake Ware from Mildenhall. But if we can establish such parameters for different contexts and problems, the great advantage of fieldwalking is that a collection exercise can be continued or repeated until the threshold which is likely to be critical has been reached, just as it may be necessary to photograph a cropmark complex on several occasions before all the attributes essential to its classification can be recorded, as Palmer (1978) has clearly demonstrated for the well-known site at Little Woodbury. Similarly, Yarwood (1980) has recently argued that lithic assemblages from peat erosion patches can only be adequately recorded if the individual exposures are continually revisited at short and regular intervals.

Achieving a sample of adequate size for a particular purpose is, of course, quite unrelated to the problem of what significance should be attached to the size of a particular sample. This is familiar in the question "how many sherds constitute (for example) a Saxon settlement?" (Foard, 1978). This is purely a problem of archaeological inference, with the answer dependent upon the cultural context and the survival potential of its artefacts. Again, experimental work may be helpful in establishing interpretational guidelines (Millett, this volume); in time it may even be possible to devise formal calibration procedures. It goes without saying that without adequate controls, the raw numbers are virtually meaningless. At the very minimum, a record of the sample fraction is essential so that the sherd density represented may be calculated. Ideally, details of the conditions under which the collection was made and the retrieval propensities of the collector should also be available, especially when results are concerned with a period such as the post-Roman horizon for which the sampled population itself is comparatively small, in order that an appropriate "weighting" can be applied whenever it seems necessary. Archaeological problems of interpretation are quite severe enough as it is without needless complications which could easily be prevented by operating a few simple controls.

The Derivation of Modern Ploughsoil Assemblages (Fig. 1.3)

As an ideal, the goal of all archaeological inference from ploughsoil assemblages can be stated very simply. Allowing for the problem that, by definition, a ploughsoil artefact is rarely in its primary depositional context, our aim is to establish what activities resulted in the deposition of that material and when? Beyond that, the task will essentially be one of consolidation. What does the presence of these activities at a particular location mean? Does it imply a permanently occupied settlement, a military or industrial site, or simply a location which was exploited at certain times for particular tasks? Within an organised community, does this suggest that specific areas had different functions—habitation, refuse disposal, etc.—or were used in different periods? As several commentators have noted (e.g. Foard, 1978; Gaffney et al., this volume) one activity which is responsible for a significant proportion of the artefacts in modern ploughsoils is the spreading of occupation refuse as manure in areas which were also cultivated in earlier periods. For this reason, amongst many others, artefacts may be deposited in the same place at very different periods although all of them eventually end up as components of the same modern ploughsoil assemblage. The problem is to be able to differentiate between them.

It is surely time archaeologists stopped sheltering behind an overworked, often almost meaningless, conceptual device—the site—as a way of evading these problems. To call a ploughsoil assemblage a "site" may be tempting for plotting distribution maps, but it tells us very little about the past. In any case, many apparent clusters derive from activities as likely to be undertaken "off-site" (Foley, 1981) as within the limits of the domestic settlement—whatever this equally unsatisfactory term actually means for a particular cultural context. If fieldwalking, and specifically surface collection, are not to continue to be branded as poor cousins of excavation, its practitioners must face up to this interpretational challenge and to the necessity of having an inferential methodology specifically tailored to the nature of their material and its peculiar problems.

To make the most of their material, as well as avoiding basic errors of interpretation, fieldworkers must apply the same sort of principles to their assemblages as do excavators to their material. What is required, in particular, is a careful consideration of the transformations through which an artefact passes between use and arrival in the deposit in which it is eventually discovered, the ploughsoil. For excavators, it is a commonplace that to explain assemblage composition, a range of factors which were instrumental in its formation need to be taken into account. These include, to name only the more obvious; cultural selection, the kind of depositional event represented, and post-depositional processes to which an artefact is subjected once it has become incorporated into the archaeological record—what Schiffer (1976) somewhat inelegantly has christened C- and N- transforms. In short, we are in the realm of what is becoming known as middle-range theory. To identify these processes, the excavator relies heavily on additional information derived from the archaeological context of a find—pit, floor surface, burial etc.,—something which is impossible in the assessment of unstratified surface material. Nevertheless, just because the latter has been subject to an additional, and particularly destructive, form of disturbance, we cannot afford to ignore the earlier stages of its depositional and post-depositional history. These are exactly comparable to those experienced by any stratified artefact, and, indeed, are the main factors accounting for the presence of ploughsoil artefacts at a particular location in space. Our

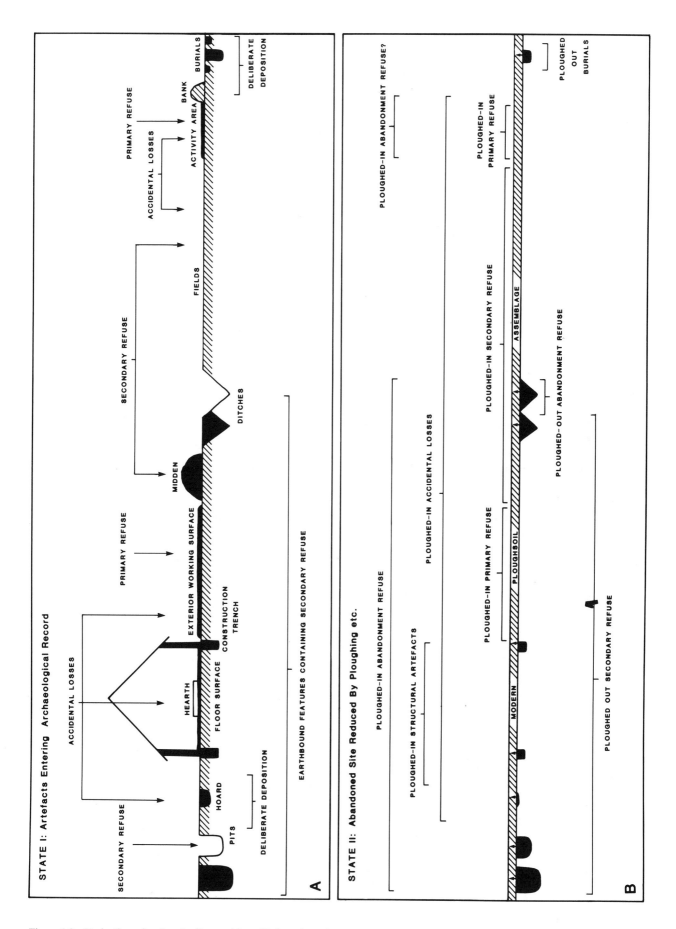

Figure 1.3   Derivation of a ploughsoil assemblage (B) for a hypothetical settlement site (A).

15

task, as in the underwater analogy mentioned previously, (Muckelroy, 1978), is to circumvent the loss of the contextual information available to the excavator and to find alternative ways of identifying these processes, based solely on properties of the artefacts and their patterns of association. The purpose of this section of the paper, is thus to give some thought to the cultural and depositional factors involved in the formation of ploughsoil assemblages, and how these might be identified—exactly the processes, in fact, which it must ultimately be our aim to understand if the interpretations we offer for surface collection are ever to be used for comparison with results from excavated sites.

A wide variety of processes are responsible for the entry of artefacts into the archaeological record and Figure 1.3A shows only some of the commonest ones, in a very simplified form. These include deliberate deposition, as with burial or the concealment of a hoard, accidental losses and refuse disposal. As Schiffer (1976) stresses, it is important to distinguish between different categories of the latter; primary refuse is discarded at its location of use, whereas secondary refuse is disposed of away from it, for example, in an old storage pit, or on the fields. Finally, there is *de facto refuse*, which is only allowed to build up when a site, or area, is being abandoned, and thus will not be related to its normal use. Only the first of these can, therefore, be used for the reconstruction of activity areas (other than refuse disposal areas). In practice, of course, the situation will be much more complex, as a result of scavenging, disturbance by later activities such as rebuilding and cleaning-out operations, when accumulations of primary refuse are removed elsewhere, effectively converting the material into secondary refuse. The assemblage eventually created by cultivation over an abandoned settlement will thus be an aggregate of all these elements, the actual composition in different areas of ploughsoil varying according to the quantities of durable artefacts contributed by each type of depositional circumstance (Fig. 1.3B).

Structural artefacts and facilities should also perhaps be mentioned here as a potential component of the ploughsoil assemblage. Technically, they can conveniently be regarded as a part of the archaeological record from the moment of completion, although for the purposes of this model, all that is important is whatever survives, after their eventual collapse or demolition, to enter the ploughsoil—most obviously items like nails or tiles, which might allow us to infer where a building had previously stood.

Reference to structures, however, draws attention to what I believe are two particularly serious misconceptions evident in the way that ploughsoil assemblages generally seem to be regarded today. Both of them at any rate, are completely at variance with the hypothetical model for ploughsoil assemblage composition which is illustrated here.

Working as we do mainly on sites which have been ploughed flat, there is first of all a tendency to forget that these sites originally existed in three dimensions above ground, as well as below it. Many—in all probability, almost all—of the activities with an archaeological residue originally took place on or above the original land surface, and only a minority of operations or tasks will have required the kind of subsoil disturbance which is responsible for the earthbound features we find on archaeological sites today. Most important of all, a great deal of the refuse which was generated must have been deposited directly on that surface and will only have been buried very gradually as new soils and sediments formed. What proportion of refuse was treated in this way will have varied according to the cultural context, but the only really significant exception to this rule is likely to have been the *re-use* of features like storage pits and ditches as refuse dumps after their abandonment from normal use. Thus, as Figure 1.3B attempts to show, it seems reasonable to regard *most* of what ends up in a cultivation horizon as effectively ploughed-*in*, rather than as ploughed-*out* of the upper layers of surviving earthbound features.

Leading on from this is a second serious misconception, which still appears in the literature all too frequently—that a connection between artefacts in the ploughsoil and other archaeological features at the same location is a probability. At its crudest, this assumption reflects our ignorance of the sheer density of archaeological material of different periods to be expected in the landscape (Foley, 1981; Schadla-Hall and Shennan, 1978). Recent work in West Yorkshire illustrates this point neatly. A series of cropmarks of types which are likely to cover the period from at least the Bronze Age to the Roman era were walked (Yarwood, 1980). All of them produced medieval pottery, and all but three, pottery of the Roman period, most of which clearly relates not to the features generating the cropmarks, but to activities at other periods, especially manuring. Flint was recovered in nearly every field searched, whether or not any cropmarks were known. Similarly, it is evident from the earlier discussion of the derivation of ploughsoil assemblages that even when earthbound features date to the same general period as artefacts in the ploughsoil, many of the latter may derive from accumulations on top of, or in, old ground surfaces, and not from primary subsoil contexts at all (Fig. 1.2B). As Crowther (1983) has already stressed, the relationship between a ploughsoil assemblage and surviving earthbound features at the same location must be a matter for investigation, not assumption.

It follows that a maxim favoured by modern policy makers must be suspect in many of the cases to which it has been applied, i.e. the argument that the more material in the subsoil, the greater the destruction of subsoil features, which interestingly, is advanced as a case both for, and against, mounting rescue excavations on cultivated sites. Much of the material in the ploughsoil, it is true, must ultimately derive from the destruction of *in situ* deposits as Figure 1.3B shows, but the onus is on those who maintain that modern cultivation is the villain of the piece to justify their contention. In cases like that of the bronze age settlement at Bishop Canning Down, there is unfortunately no doubt whatever that it was (Gingell and Schadla-Hall, 1980), but in many others, most of what is *already* in the ploughsoil may be survivals from much earlier agricultural operations, and the proportion contributed by modern erosion from earthbound features negligible. Again, experimental controls are needed. The subsoil surface under old field boundaries can be investigated as a measure of the erosion due to agriculture in adjacent areas, as at Barton Court Farm, where the gravel surface survived 5–10 cm. higher at the edge of the fields. A cruder measure could be the incidence of less robust pottery fabrics on the surface, compared with their representation in excavated contexts on similar sites in the area, although this would obviously require some difficult assumptions. With lithic assemblages, microwear studies (Holgate, this volume) should be capable of establishing whether material has been subject to very long periods of cultivation. Ultimately, however, the moral is simple. If the erosion of subsoil features is considered a problem, the rate at which it occurs must be established directly, and not through proxy indicators such as the quantity of artefacts in the ploughsoil.

A corollary of the points which have just been made is that many "sites" *never* had any significant earthbound features—not just hunter/gatherer camps and temporary activity areas, but also quite possibly permanent settlements in various later periods, such as the early Neolithic or the earlier Bronze Age to name two of the obvious. If this is so, then the only evidence for the core of the settlement pattern still surviving in intensively cultivated areas is likely to be in the form of lithic scatters. However unpromising these seem at first glance, careful study of the assemblage, e.g. its differentiation into functional types, may yield important clues about the nature of various activities carried out on these sites (Holgate, this volume). There may even be a case for the total *excavation* of various types of ploughsoil scatters to ascertain the total assemblage variability and evidence of any spatial patterning which might suggest where different tasks were actually performed.

On account of their aggregate composition, behavioural interpretation of ploughsoil assemblages will always be an exceptionally difficult task. For this reason, investigation of the spatial patterning of different classes of artefacts is likely to be the most productive approach to individual sites or artefact clusters. Two kinds of distributional trends can be particularly helpful in indicating when different parts of a site were in use, and for what purpose: significant differences between types of artefacts, or a clear pattern of covariation. If necessary, the patterning can be investigated mathematically using a variety of the well-tried tests of spatial association which are available (Muckelroy, 1978).

Determining the nature of different parts of a site from a ploughsoil assemblage presupposes the existence of a suitable classificatory framework for dividing artefacts into different functional categories, as well as demanding the exercise of considerable ingenuity in its application. To date there has been next to no work on this problem, although Crowther (pers. comm.) suggests that dividing artefacts along the following lines could be a useful preliminary exercise: (1) structural artefacts, (2) tools and equipment, (3) personal artefacts, (4) societal artefacts, (such as coins), and (5) unclassified. With the commoner classes of material a much greater degree of refinement is clearly possible. Pottery fabrics for example could be differentiated according to whether they represent finewares, everyday wares, or heavy-duty vessels. Such a division is inevitably highly subjective, but even so, can lead to interesting results. In the case of one of the Aisne Valley sites, *BLG* (Fig. 1.2A), table-wares are concentrated near the centre of the site, in the vicinity of what seems to be the major Roman buildings, whereas the heavier storage vessels, and amphorae seem to have been discarded primarily around the fringes of this area. Further discussion of these classificatory problems is needed.

Work on excavated sites has demonstrated conclusively that not only the nature of material, but also the way it has been treated, may provide invaluable information on the activities taking place in different areas. Most animal bone, for example, is discarded at one of three stages—after butchery, after food preparation or after eating—and it is sometimes possible to relate debris to one or other of those actions, according to which parts of the carcass are represented (Halstead *et al.*, 1978). At the iron age site of Wendon's Ambo in Essex, meat bones were concentrated in the core settlement area, whereas around the edges of the site, the percentage of limb bones was much higher in a pattern markedly reminiscent of the *BLG* pottery distribution. Unfortunately animal bone is rarely likely to survive in ploughsoil in sufficient quantity for such an exercise to be attempted. It is, however, a pointer to what might be done with altogether more robust materials such as pottery or lithic tools and debitage, just as it goes without saying that the evidence of patterns of association can be enhanced by data drawn from ancillary investigations e.g. phosphate or magnetometer surveys. An obvious extension of this line of work will be to examine the relationship between patterns of refuse disposal within sites and the kind of material used to manure the fields. At Wendon's Ambo, a relationship between the debris concentrated around the periphery of the settlement and the latter activity seems not improbable (*cf.* Halstead *et al.*, 1978). More work on manuring practices in general as well as in different cultural and regional contexts, is obviously needed, not least because one consequence of certain classes of material constantly being removed in this manner will be to alter the composition of the asemblage remaining to be recovered within the confines of the settlement. For the study of economic questions such as marketing patterns, this can be crucial since it

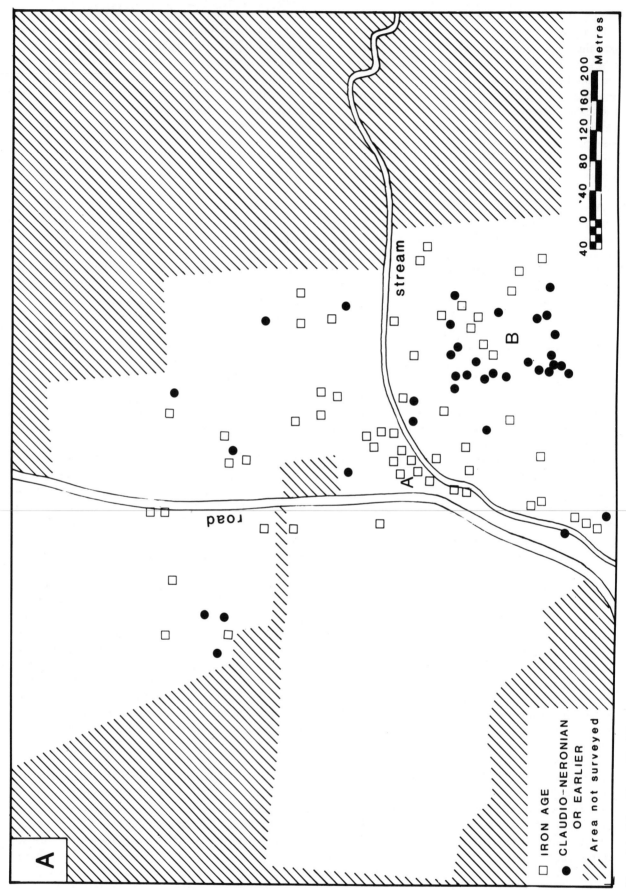

Figure 1.4 Saham Toney, Norfolk: distribution of Iron Age and Roman coins (A) Pre-Flavian (B) Flavian to Hadrianic.

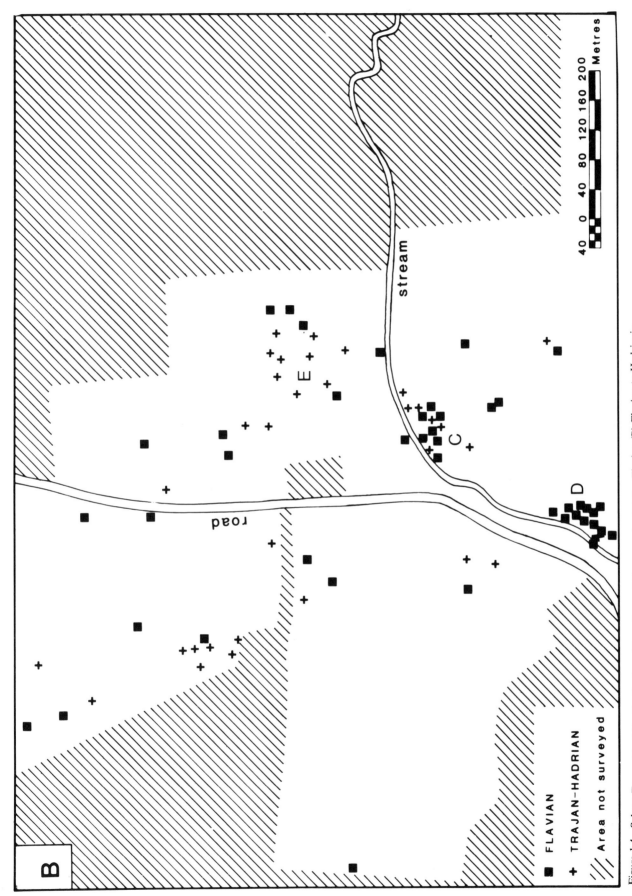

Figure 1.4   Saham Toney, Norfolk: distribution of Iron Age and Roman coins (A) Pre-Flavian (B) Flavian to Hadrianic.

19

immediately unbalances any comparisons between an agricultural site and other categories of settlement like towns or forts, where we are uncertain whether or not the bulk of the rubbish was dumped within the site.

As was remarked earlier, archaeologists have been relatively slow to exploit the obvious potential of surface collection for making detailed comparisons between sites of the same general period. Providing this is effected using ploughsoil artefact samples standing alone, and in terms of uniform measures of assemblage variation such as density or relative frequencies, the process should be relatively straightforward. Problems start to occur, however, as soon as comparison with an excavated assemblage is contemplated, owing to the more comprehensive nature of the latter with regard to less durable artefact types. For any comparative exercise to be valid, then *like* must be compared with *like*. This, in turn, effectively requires omitting from consideration any components of the excavated sample which could not reasonably be expected to survive plough action and exposure on a cultivated site. What we are aiming to be left with, in fact, is a kind of lowest common denominator.

It has to be admitted that in the present state of knowledge, this is by no means easy to determine, nor will it be until experimental data, such as that planned by Reynolds and Schadla-Hall (1980), becomes available. For the present, we can only make the fullest possible use of anything diagnostic which survives in sufficient quantities to generate an assemblage with a composition that reflects spatial and temporal processes; anything, in fact, which can be readily dated. Ideally it will also have a known source. Which artefact types are the best indicators naturally varies according to the regional and cultural context—for the Roman period, they may be anything from finewares like *terra sigillata* and amphorae, to coins and brooches, whereas before the Iron Age, they are likely to be one form of lithic implement or another. A further practical consideration is the ease of obtaining an adequate sample to answer whatever questions are being posed. In the case of the Aisne Valley, one such problem is the proportion of amphora fabrics from Italian and Spanish sources present on late iron age and early Gallo-Roman sites. Determining this for a large fortified settlement like Pommiers, can be a matter of an hour's work, whereas for most of the rural sites, a greater investment of time and labour will certainly be needed (Haselgrove, 1983). Obtaining sufficient quantities of artefacts like brooches or coins could take years of assiduous searching.

The dividends from long-term programmes can, however, be enormous as the results from an extensive iron age and Roman rural settlement at Saham Toney, Norfolk clearly shows (Fig. 1.4). The site is under intensive cultivation, and has also been badly disturbed by dredging operations in the valley bottom. As a result of intensive fieldwalking carried out over several years, more than 700 iron age and Roman coins have now been recovered as well as quantities of other artefacts such as brooches, military equipment and pottery (R.A. Brown, pers. comm.). In each case, the findspot was carefully recorded. Originally the site was believed to be an extensive Roman rural settlement of a well-known type, but from plotting the dateable artefacts, it has become clear that the internal development of the site is rather more complex, taking place, it may be suggested, along the following lines:

1. The growth of a pre-Roman settlement nucleus in the valley bottom (Fig. 1.4A:A), where La Tène I and La Tène II brooches and so-called "coin moulds" have been found, as well as quantities of the local Icenian silver coinage
2. The establishment of a Claudio-Neronian fort on rising ground to the south of the stream which overlooks this settlement area, represented by a cluster of early coins, military equipment, etc. (Fig. 1.4A:B)
3. When Roman coinage begins to be found in the civilian settlement area, it is to the south of the original nucleus (Fig. 1.4B:C), suggesting a possible break or shift in occupation. There is also a probable scattered hoard further south along the course of the stream (Fig. 1.4B:D)
4. In the later first and second centuries AD, a gradual expansion of the settlement northwards from the original nucleus (Fig. 1.4B:E).

Among one of the most interesting possibilities raised by the overall coin distribution is that the indigenous silver coinage remained in circulation for much longer than is generally accepted, i.e. well into the second century AD, although alternative explanations for this patterning are obviously plausible. Nevertheless, the implications are clear enough. No cropmark evidence for this site is forthcoming, although it has been sought on numerous occasions. Yet as a result of this intensive fieldwalking survey, we already possess a lot of information about the site. Should a research excavation be contemplated, this will provide a valuable framework for the investigation; if not, and in the meantime, we already possess a basis for understanding the history of the site and a means of comparing it with others in the region and beyond.

Conclusions: Some Cautionary Tales from the Aisne Valley, France

The Aisne Valley survey has already been mentioned on several occasions, and is outlined in detail in the interim report on the first season's work (Haselgrove, 1983). In brief, the aim is a greater understanding of the iron age and Gallo-Roman settlement pattern, with particular emphasis on the development of major nucleated settlements like Pommiers, Vieux-Reims and Villeneuve-St-Germain at the close of the first millennium BC. A multi-stage survey design has been adopted, involving as a first step, characterisation of a number of known sites spanning the period of interest by means of surface collection, and as a control, the excavation of an iron age and Gallo-Roman rural site at Beaurieux Les Grèves *(BLG)*. The aim of this work, a necessary preliminary to the programme, was to set levels of expectation for the next stage, the definition of new sites and clusters, through the intensive survey of a number of sample units chosen to be representative of the geography and topography of the region. Much of the work undertaken in 1983 was of an experimental nature, e.g. determining an effective spacing of fieldwalkers for the recognition of artefact clusters in areas under intensive cultivation, and will not be discussed further here. I should, however, like to comment briefly on results relating to some of the main theories addressed in this paper, firstly, distortions arising out of differential recovery by individual workers, or the way the results are presented and how these problems can be overcome; and secondly, the value of ploughsoil assemblages for detecting intra-site patterning and inter-site comparison.

I Recovery and presentation problems

As already mentioned, a systematic surface collection by 10 m. squares was undertaken in 1983, over part of the known cropmark site at *BLG*. After the first four squares walked had produced over 200 sherds, the sampling fraction was reduced to 50%. The results indicated a distinct concentration of iron age material, with contemporary imports such as Dressel 1A and B amphorae, to the north of the modern track bisecting the site (Fig. 1.5A), while for the Roman period two clusters are apparent (Fig. 1.5B), one of them potentially related to the major cropmark features in the centre of the site (also Fig. 1.6A). On the basis of this evidence, together with that of the cropmarks, and the results of the resistivity survey, trial excavations were mounted with very useful results (Haselgrove, 1983).

Despite the success of the excavation, retrospective consideration of the surface collection results suggests that they are, in actual fact, potentially highly misleading, and that this is a function of differential recovery rates, and the manner in which they were initially presented. One factor in this is evidently the masking effect of heavy stubble cover in one of the two parcels of land north of the track, and coverage of that area was quickly suspended for that very reason. It must be considered highly probable that the existence of the track has similar effects on the units which it bisects (Fig. 1.5C), which then seemingly calls into question the existence of two separate concentrations of Roman material.

Far more worrying, however, is the possibility raised by the overall distribution of sherds from the survey area (Fig. 1.5C) that the clustering effect is entirely spurious and a product of individuals' recovery rates. The collection was carried out in two blocks, one of which (Zone A) was walked by an experienced team working in an unhurried manner, whereas the other (Zone B) was walked by a new team freshly arrived from England in the short space of time left to complete the exercise. Although the latter seemed to collect just as much tile as the first group, their recovery of pottery was minimal: only 94 sherds as against over 700. Was this a reflection of Team B not having had time to acclimatise and get used to the conditions, or was there a genuine diminution in the quantity of pottery in this part of the site?

In order to clarify this point, it is evidently necessary to investigate these results further, and to do so, the average sherd weight for each square has been calculated as a rough measure of the recovery rate of individual workers. The assumption behind this method of evaluation is simply that the better the recovery rate, the greater the quantity of smaller sherds which will be present in the sample. The results are divided into size classes from 1 (the smallest) to 5 (the largest) and are set out in Tables 1.1 and 1.2; ∞ indicates that no sherds were recovered (quite possibly because there were none). Making due allowances for the crudeness of the method, these results must be considered highly suggestive.

Table 1.1 shows the cumulative achievement of the two teams. What is notable here (as well as gratifying) is the consistency of the results obtained by the experienced workers, only one '4' being recorded (and that from outside the area of the cropmarks) when all fabrics in the sample are taken into account. The results for iron age fabrics alone are clearly not quite as good but, allowing for the fact that they form only a minority of the assemblage, are perfectly acceptable. In contrast, the results of Team B are clearly far more variable, and much of the pottery which they collected was in the upper end of the size range.

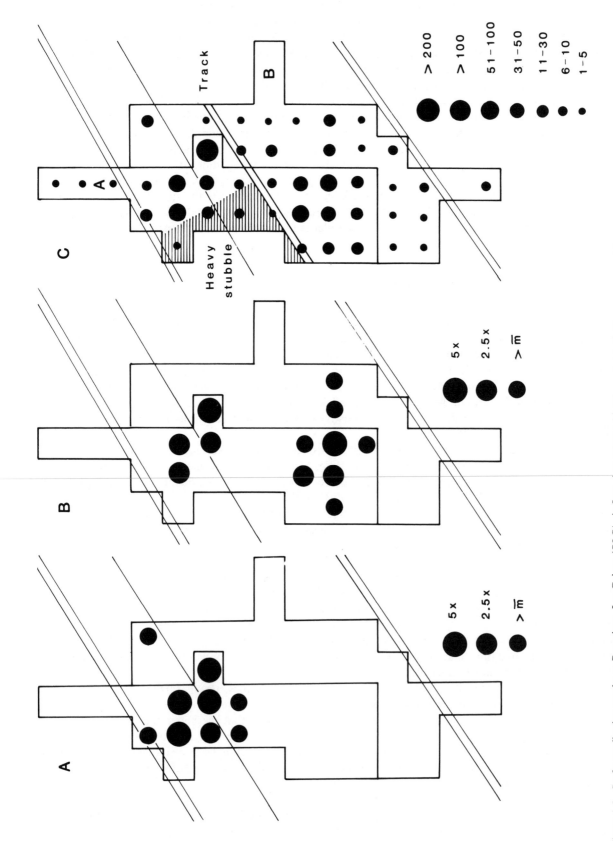

Figure 1.5 Surface collection results at Beaurieux, Les Grèves (*BLG*). A: Iron Age pottery (sherd numbers); B: Roman pottery (sherd numbers); C: Total sherd recovery (sherd numbers).

When the results are retabulated according to individuals' scores, this only serves to confirm the impression that the results have been heavily influenced by each worker's performance (Table 1.2). While some people may just have been plain unlucky in their choice of squares, others clearly had difficulty in picking out the smaller sherds; hardly surprising given the dry conditions, the nature of the local fabrics and the sheer density of tile all over the site. A further point well worth noting is the performance of individuals 1 and 3 in group A, which fell markedly for the squares which they walked after they had assumed responsibility for supervising Group B, just as one would predict, given the demands of writing labels and assigning workers to a new square which are constantly being made of those in charge, a factor, I would like to think, contributing to the relatively inconsistent performance of individual 4! On the other hand, the speed at which individuals worked does not seem to have had any great effect on their performance, the results obtained by those who covered most squares apparently being broadly comparable with the figures achieved by those who covered less.

Table 1.1: Efficiency of sherd recovery from two surface collection units at Beaurieux, Les Grèves (*BLG*), based on mean size of sherds recovered.

Zone A			Zone B		
Score	Frequency of each score recorded		Score	Frequency of each score recorded	
	All fabrics	Iron Age fabrics		All fabrics	Iron Age fabrics
1	1	1	1	0	0
2	16	9	2	4	1
3	6	4	3	3	4
4	1	3	4	7	0
5	0	1	5	4	1
∞	0	6	∞	8	21

∞ Indicates no sherds recovered from a 20 m. square.

Table 1.2: Efficiency of individuals' sherd recovery from two surface collection units at Beaurieux, Les Grèves (*BLG*), based on mean size of sherds recovered.

	Zone A					Zone B							
All Fabrics													
Individual	1	2	3	4	5	6	7	8	9	10	11	12	13
Score													
1	-	-	-	1*	-	-	-	-	-	-	-	-	-
2	3	5	2	2*	5	2	1	-	-	-	1	-	-
3	2	1	3	2*	1	-	-	-	-	1	-	-	-
4	2*	-	-	1*	-	1	2	1	-	-	-	1	1
5	1*	-	1*	-	-	1	-	-	-	-	-	-	1
∞	-	-	-	-	-	2	1	1	1	2	1	-	-
Iron Age Fabrics													
1	-	-	-	1*	-	-	-	-	-	-	-	-	-
2	1	3	2	2*	2	-	1	-	-	-	-	-	-
3	1	2	2*	-	2	-	1	-	-	-	-	-	1
4	1	-	1	-	2	-	-	-	-	-	-	-	-
5	1*	-	1*	1*	-	1	-	-	-	-	-	-	-
∞	5*	-	2	2*	-	5	2	2	1	3	2	1	1

* Includes results obtained while supervising volunteers.

∞ Indicates no sherds recovered from a 20m. square.

Individual performance, therefore, can clearly influence recovery, which raises the question of how to overcome any resultant distortion in the presentation of material from surface collection procedures. A number of possibilities present themselves, making use of relative quantities; in the investigation of spatial patterning it is, after all, the relative differences between units which are important rather than the absolute value. Two are used here. In the case of *BLG*, the biggest single source of variation is clearly the differential recovery rate of the two teams. The results for Roman sherd numbers given in Figure 1.5B have, therefore, been replotted using two separate means for the two zones, but the same interval measures of relative density (Fig. 1.6B). This alters the pattern quite noticeably, incidentally bringing it closer in line with the impression suggested by the concentrations of tile (Fig. 1.6A). The alternative method, which is to work in terms of the relative proportions of different fabrics from individual squares, has been applied to the iron age material (Fig. 1.6C). This seems to confirm that the absence of iron age pottery from Zone B is a genuine trend, although the results have to be used with care, and in conjunction with the absolute quantities given in Figure 1.5A, as the

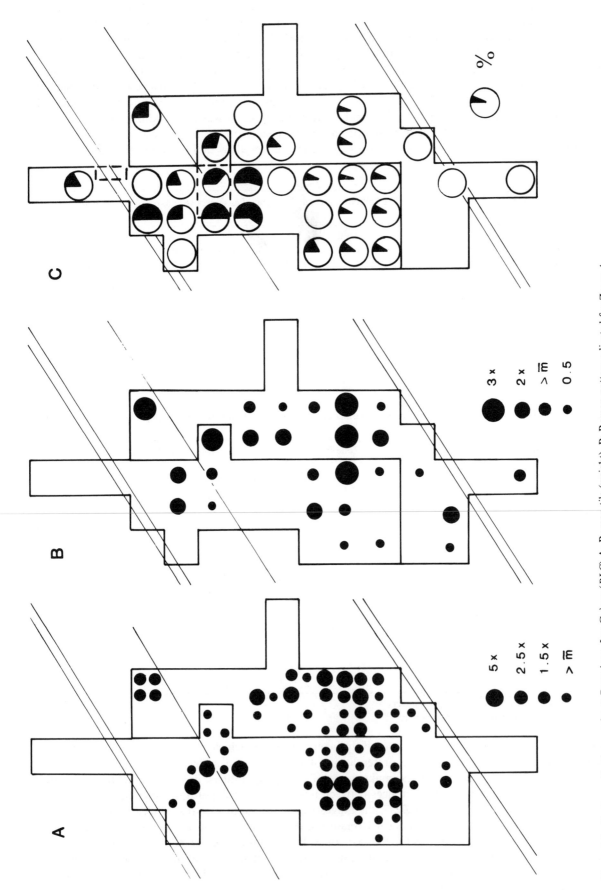

Figure 1.6   Surface collection results at Beaurieux, Les Grèves (*BLG*) A: Roman tile (weight), B: Roman pottery adjusted for Zones A and B (sherd numbers), C: Proportion of Iron Age pottery per 20 m. square (sherd numbers). Dotted lines indicate areas of excavation.

figures will also be dependent on variations in the density of Roman pottery across the site. It will be obvious that many of these "iron age" fabrics continued in use alongside the Romanised assemblage, a possibility which would seem to be substantiated by their presence as a small, but consistent, proportion of the major Roman cluster in the centre of the site. But there appear to be no grounds for rejecting the hypothesis that the main locus of Iron Age activity is to be found to the north of the modern track, a consideration which is of paramount importance in planning further stages of the investigation of this site.

II Intra- and inter-site variation: preliminary results

One of the primary considerations of undertaking the excavation at *BLG* is to provide the project with a detailed understanding of an iron age and Gallo-Roman farmstead on the Aisne gravels, which can be used as a control in the evaluation of surface collection results from other known sites in similar locations, or as a yardstick against which sites newly discovered by field-walking may be assessed. Thus, while the results of the excavation will obviously be of importance *per se* for the information they can be expected to give us on such matters as the development of the settlement, the subsistence practices of its inhabitants and their economic relations with the major nucleated sites, a paramount consideration in the exercise is to work out just *what* could safely be inferred:

1. from the results of the surface collection alone
2. from the results of the surface collection taken in conjunction with the the cropmark evidence, and
3. from the results of surface collection, considered alongside those produced by other non-destructive methods of investigation such as geophysical and phosphate surveys.

In other words, given certain basic assumptions about regularities in human behaviour in the region during the Iron Age and the Gallo-Roman period, it is hoped that the results will be able to add a certain amount of *detail* to the interpretation of other sites in the area for which the only forms of evidence are ploughsoil assemblages and cropmarks. For this reason, as in the work undertaken by Crowther (1983) at Maxey, the relationship between the ploughsoil assemblages and subsoil finds is to be a matter of intensive investigation at all stages of the excavation at *BLG*.

While it is obviously too early for a detailed picture to have emerged, one or two of the preliminary results can be mentioned as they are highly relevant to the argument advanced earlier in the paper. While the detailed work on the composition of assemblages from excavated contexts has yet to be completed, it is already clear that there is no obvious or simple relationship between features. The square over the two outer enclosure ditches, (Fig. 1.6C) yielded virtually no surface material, despite the fact that both of these contained significant quantities of robust late iron age fabrics. There is, however, material from both immediately inside and immediately outside the line of these ditches. This should not, therefore, be a matter of horizontal displacement, and in any case, the ground is level. A more likely explanation would seem to be dumping of refuse first beyond the limits of the enclosure, and then after the abandonment of this ditch system, around the periphery of the smaller enclosure which seems to have supplanted it (Haselgrove, 1983). A clue to this may be the comparative rarity of storage pits or other large features which could be used for rubbish on these gravel terrace settlements, necessitating its disposal at the enclosure limits, or as manure beyond them.

The picture from the main area excavated so far seems very similar (Fig. 1.6C). Despite the concentration of iron age pottery in the ploughsoil, underlying it boundary features predominate: the ditches of the smaller enclosure and, predating these, palisade trenches belonging to the settlement phases of the Mid-Late Iron Age and the Late Bronze–Earlier Iron Age respectively. The latter is apparently unrepresented in the ploughsoil assemblage, presumably a reflection of the friability of the contemporary ceramics. If not marking the limits of settlement areas, these features are certainly suggestive of significant internal partitions. It seems highly probable that the core of the habitation for all these phases lies slightly to the south-west, an area which it is planned to examine in 1984. It is interesting, given the high proportion of iron age pottery in the ploughsoil (36% in a sample of 80 sherds), that significantly different results were obtained from an excavated sample of it, ploughsoil remaining after machine clearance which was cleaned off by trowel. In this, the proportion was as low as 8% (in a sample of 156 sherds) and is to be explained in one of two ways: the grog in the fabric of a very common iron age storage vessel type perhaps giving its sherds rather greater visibility on the surface in comparison with the Romanised wares or, rather more likely, over-enthusiastic scraping of the surface of earthbound features of Roman date during the cleaning operation. There will have to be further investigations of these questions.

Although in our present state of knowledge, a relationship between the clustering of iron age material and areas located at the periphery of the various pre-Roman settlement phases seems not improbable, there are other possibilities which we cannot afford to overlook. This is particularly true when the focus of a settlement has shifted, as seems to have been the case at *BLG*. In such cases, much of the material in the ploughsoil may derive from whatever deposits accumulated at the time of the move: in other words, it could reflect the abandonment process, Schiffer's (1976) *de facto* refuse. Alternatively, it could relate to its use for rubbish disposal after the move was completed, although at *BLG* we can safely discard this latter possibility in view of the way the Roman material is patterned.

I refer here to the sharp division in the total *terra sigillata* assemblage from the site. Although the sample is small (only 24 identifiable sherds), the pattern is so clear cut (Fig. 1.7), with such a high proportion of the early South Gaulish pottery coming from the cluster to the north of the modern track, and almost all the later fabrics from the southern concentration, that the results can be accepted at face value. This evidence, in turn, is extremely useful in reinforcing the pattern implied by other material, such as amphorae, and has not been contradicted so far by the excavations when there would otherwise be a temptation to postulate an expansion of the settlement area during the Gallo-Roman period from the surface assemblage rather than displacement (Figs. 1.5–1.6).

Although not so clear cut, the pattern at Limé, Les Terres Noires (*LTN*) also gives indications of a relatively complex history of settlement development (Fig. 1.7). The total site assemblage is closely comparable to the later of the two clusters at *BLG*, but within the site, activity seems to begin in the east and to last longest in the central of the three concentrations of material (Fig. 1.2B). The apparent dominance of Central Gaulish fabric in the western part of the site may be an anomaly stemming from the very small sample available, a reminder that although in terms of density there is no reason not to suppose the distinction genuine, further collection will be needed to generate a sample size adequate for the other facets of inter-site comparison. Some doubt must also attach to the autonomy of the easternmost cluster, which could simply reflect clearance of material to the edge of the field, although at present its priority seems to be substantiated by the iron age material from the site. There is certainly no reason to suppose *LTN* a Roman foundation: the total quantity of South-Gaulish fabric is as high from *BLG* from a much smaller sample fraction, and the reason it forms such a small proportion of the total could simply be a reflection of the overall quantity of South-Gaulish material circulating in the area, compounded by a subsequent change in the status and size of the site compared to *BLG*. Further work on this problem will be undertaken in the future. In general terms, this pattern of a shift in the focus of rural settlements sometime after the Roman conquest is an interesting one, as it also appears possible for some of the other known cropmark sites in the region, where Romanised buildings can be made out standing adjacent to enclosures of the type commonly known as *fermes indigènes* and assumed mostly to be of later iron age date, e.g. on the plateau north of Soissons.

In general terms, *terra sigillata* is clearly among the most useful components of the ploughsoil assemblage for investigating both intra- and inter-site variation in the Gallo-Roman period. Other things being equal, it has a relatively good chance of consistent recovery by different individuals, and can be relatively easily subdivided by fabric into groupings which have both geographical and (some) chronological significance. At the inter-site level, even these small *terra sigillata* samples from *BLG* and *LTN* represent a welcome addition in an area of northern France where there are still very few quantifiable assemblages which have been published. Marsh (1981), in fact, uses only four. Unfortunately both Aisne Valley sites seem to bear out his assertion that the region as a whole suffered an acute shortage of *terra sigillata* in the early second century AD, which clearly affects the utility of these assemblages as a chronological tool.

It is comment enough on current *lacunae* in our knowledge when the domination of these two assemblages by East Gaulish fabrics has to be admitted as one of their most significant features. This is precisely what one would expect from the geographical location of the Aisne Valley in relation to the kiln areas, but not a trend which is evident as yet in any published data (*cf*. Marsh, 1981). In fact, the closest parallel to the two assemblages, on Marsh's data, are *Limes* forts in Holland and Switzerland, which is patently absurd. The results also serve to underline Millett's *caveat* that the proportion of East Gaulish fabric is often misrepresented in comparison with the others because it has been calculated on the basis of decorated and stamped vessels alone, (which are less common in East Gaulish ware), rather than from the total site assemblage as it should have been (Millett, 1980). If this is so, it is a deficiency perhaps best remedied by the collection of fresh information. The above results must be grounds for optimism that surface collection can often be a fast and effective alternative to excavation, for doing just that. In any case, without systematic survey and reliable quantifiable data from all the different types of site, it is hard to see how studies of the regional economy can ever be put on a sound footing, an observation which can be extended to almost every conceivable aspect of archaeological settlement studies and all periods.

Summary

Inevitably, much of this paper has focussed on the difficulties of interpreting ploughsoil assemblages, and, as yet, only very tentative ideas can be offered for overcoming most of them. Nevertheless, it is to be hoped that

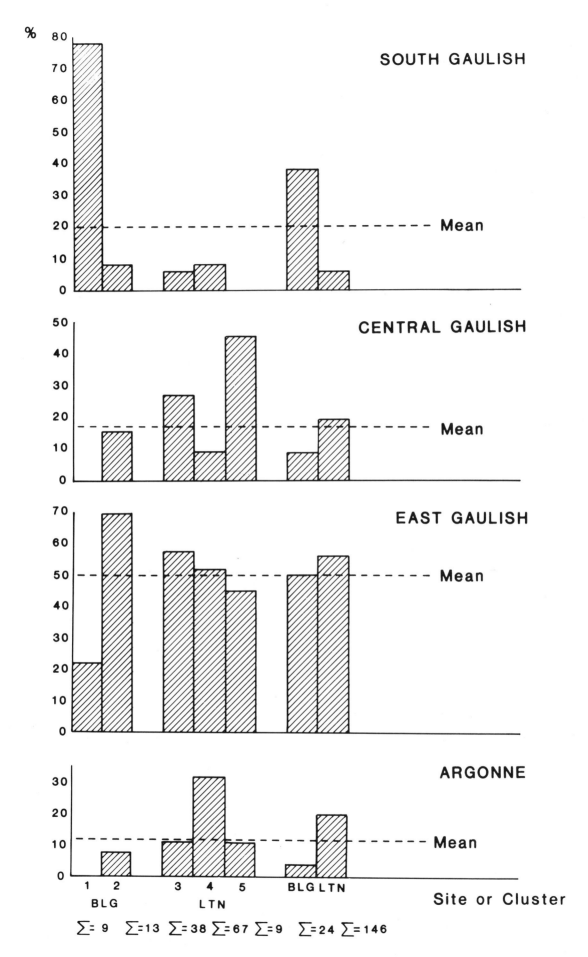

Figure 1.7 Proportions of *terra sigillata* fabrics from Beaurieux, Les Grèves (*BLG*) and Limé, Les Terres Noires (*LTN*).

by making some of these problems more explicit, others active in fieldwork and surface collection will be stimulated to consider new possibilities for their material, and to experiment with ways of controlling and calibrating it. Only by doing so will we gradually be able to build up a framework which will allow us to place any real confidence in fieldwalking results. Yet this is essential, given the ubiquity of modern cultivation and the inadequacy of archaeological resources for exploring all aspects of the past in the detail we should like. Both in their own right, and for the extra dimension of understanding they can bring to many problems, fieldwork data are already of the utmost importance, and can only become more so. If their potential is to be exploited to the full, more rigorous inferential procedures are necessary, and we must set about devising them without further delay.

Acknowledgements

Discussions with many people have contributed to the ideas presented in this paper, especially David Crowther and Martin Millett. I should like to thank them, together with Robin Brown for generously allowing me to make use of the results of his work at Saham Toney, Andrew Fitzpatrick for his identification of the Aisne Valley pottery, and Yvonne Brown and Pam Lowther for their work on the illustrations which accompany the article. I should also like to record my gratitude to all those who assisted in the 1983 programme of fieldwork in France.

Since the volume went to press, the final report on Stephen Shennan's (1985) East Hampshire Survey, in which many of these problems were made the subject of detailed investigation, has now been published, and ought to be consulted by anyone concerned with the theory and practice of field survey.

Bibliography

Cherry, J.F., Gamble, C. and Shennan, S. (eds.) 1978 *Sampling in Contemporary British Archaeology*. Oxford: British Archaeological Reports British Series 50

Clarke, D.V. 1979 Excavation and volunteers: a cautionary tale. *World Archaeology* 10: 63–70

Cowgill, G. 1975 A selection of samplers: archaeo-statistics. In *Sampling in Archaeology*, J.W. Mueller (ed.) pp. 258–274. Tucson: University of Arizona Press

Crowther, D. 1981 Metal detectors at Maxey. *Current Archaeology* 77: 172–176

Crowther, D. 1983 Old land surfaces and modern ploughsoil: implications of recent work at Maxey, Cambs. *Scotttish Archaeological Review* 2: 31–44

Doran, J.E. and Hodson, F.R. 1975 *Mathematics and Computers in Archaeology*. Edinburgh: Edinburgh University Press

Foard, G. 1978 Systematic fieldwalking and the investigation of Saxon settlement in Northamptonshire. *World Archaeology* 9: 357–374

Foard, G. 1980 The recovery of archaeological information by systematic fieldwalking: research in Northamptonshire and Bedfordshire. In *Fieldwalking as a Method of Archaeological Research*. C. Hayfield (ed.). pp. 34–40. London: DOE. (Occasional Paper 2)

Foley, R.A. 1981 Off-site archaeology: an alternative approach for the short-sited. In *Pattern of the Past*, I.R. Hodder, G. Isaac and N. Hammond (eds.) pp.157–182. Cambridge: Cambridge University Press

Gingell, C. 1980 The Marlborough Downs in the Bronze Age. In *Settlement and Society in the British Later Bronze Age*. J. Barrett and R. Bradley (eds.): pp. 209–222 Oxford: British Archaeological Reports British Series 83

Gingell, C. and Schadla-Hall, R.T. 1980 Excavations at Bishop's Canning Down, 1976. In *The Past Under the Plough*. J. Hinchliffe and R.T. Schadla-Hall (eds.) pp. 109–113. London: DOE (Occasional Paper 3)

Halstead, P., Hodder, I.R. and Jones, G. 1978 Behavioural archaeology and refuse patterns: a case study. *Norwegian Archaeological Review* 11: 118–131

Haselgrove, C.C. 1983 *La Vallée de L'Aisne, France, 1983: An Interim Report*. Durham

Hayfield, C. 1980 *Fieldwalking as a method of Archaeological Research*. London: DOE (Occasional Paper 2)

Hinchliffe, J. and Schadla-Hall, R.T. (eds.) 1980 *The Past under the Plough*. London: DOE (Occasional Paper 3)

Hodder, I.R. 1974 The distribution of Savernake Ware. *Wiltshire Archaeology Magazine* 69: 67–84

Lambrick, G. 1977 *Archaeology and Agriculture*. Oxford: Oxford Archaeological Unit (Survey 4)

Marsh, G. 1981 London's Samian supply and its relationship to the development of the Gallic Samian industry. In *Roman Pottery Research in Britain and North-west Europe*, A.C. and A.S. Anderson (eds.) pp. 173–238 Oxford: British Archaeological Reports British Series 123

Miles, D. 1980 Some comments on the effects of agriculture in the Upper Thames Valley. In *The Past Under the Plough*. J. Hinchliffe and R.T. Schadla-Hall (eds.) pp. 78–81. London: DOE (Occasional Paper 3)

Millett, M.J. 1980 Aspects of Romano-British pottery in West Sussex. *Sussex Archaeological Collections* 118: 57–68

Millett, M.J. 1983 *A Comparative Study of some Contemporaneous Pottery Assemblages from Roman Britain*. D. Phil. Thesis, University of Oxford: Unpublished

Muckelroy, K.W. 1978 *Maritime Archaeology*. Cambridge: Cambridge University Press

Palmer, R. 1978 Aerial Archaeology and sampling. In *Sampling in Contemporary British Archaeology* J.F. Cherry, C. Gamble and S. Shennan (eds.) pp. 129–148. Oxford: British Archaeological Reports British Series 50

Reynolds, P.J. and Schadla-Hall, R.T. 1980 Measurement of plough-damage and the effects of plough-damage on archaeological material. In *The Past Under the Plough*. J. Hinchliffe and R.T. Schadla-Hall (eds.) pp. 114–119. London: DOE (Occasional Paper 3)

Schadla-Hall, R.T. and Shennan, S. 1978 Some suggestions for a sampling approach to archaeological survey in Wessex. In *Sampling in Contemporary British Archaeology*. J.F. Cherry, C. Gamble and S. Shennan (eds.) pp. 87–104. Oxford: British Archaeological Reports British Series 50

Schiffer, M.B. 1976 *Behavioural Archaeology* New York: Academic Press

Shennan, S. 1985 *Experiments in the Collection and Analysis of Archaeological Survey Data: The East Hampshire Survey*. Sheffield: Department of Archaeology and Prehistory

Woodward. P. 1978 A problem-orientated approach to the recovery of knapped flint debris: a fieldwalking strategy for answering questions posed by the site distributions and excavations. In *Sampling in Contemporary British Archaeology*. J.F. Cherry, C. Gamble and S. Shennan (eds.) pp. 121–128. Oxford: British Archaeological Reports British Series 50

Yarwood, R.E. 1980 The organisation and purpose of fieldwalking in West Yorkshire. In *Fieldwalking as a Method of Archaeological Research*. C. Hayfield (ed.) pp. 20–25. London: DOE (Occasional Paper 2)

2. Field Survey Calibration : a Contribution

by Martin Millett

Most discussions of the results of archaeological surveys now pay at least lip-service to the post-depositional factors which have transformed the evidence. Less attention is however paid to the equally important culturally determined factors which govern how much material is deposited in different periods and therefore available for discovery. Whilst most archaeologists are aware that the amount of material culture in circulation varies between societies, there has beeen little attempt to quantify this, or to make allowance for it in the interpretation of gross distribution patterns.

It is the purpose of this paper to suggest that it is by measuring the amount of material culture appearing in specific dated contexts on excavations that we can begin to establish what a surface distribution of similar material means. The fact that most of the data used in this study is pottery, should not be taken to suggest that a similar methodology ought not to be used for other artefacts.

At its crudest, anyone who has excavated a Saxon settlement knows that pottery is rarer on them than on similar sites of, for instance, the Roman period. Despite this no-one seems to have attempted to quantify this, or use it to calibrate the information from survey. The practical problem which confronts those wishing to try this is the absence of suitable data. Whilst enlightened pottery specialists quantify their data, they almost never indicate what volume of earth was removed to produce that quantity of pottery. Such data need to be made available for a variety of sites with a wide geographical and chronological range, so that the range of variation can be established.

The information presented here is only a first step towards this, as it derives from only two sites, although these do illustrate some of the pitfalls of such data. The first set of information is that relating to the number of sherds per-unit-volume excavated from a medieval and post-medieval sequence at Bath Orange Grove. This site was excavated by Tim O'Leary for Bath Archaeological Trust, and the pottery report has been prepared by Jeremy Evans and the author (see O'Leary, forthcoming). Tim O'Leary kindly provided data on the excavated volume of each phase, and these have been grouped together into a series of time units. The results are shown in Table 2.1 and Figure 2.1.

Table 2.1: Number of Sherds per-unit-volume excavated at Bath Orange Grove, (from O'Leary, forthcoming).

	15th Century	16th Century	early 17th Century	late 17th Century
All sherds	23.6	10.4	4.4	10.9
Non-residual sherds only	1.7	3.2	1.6	10.9

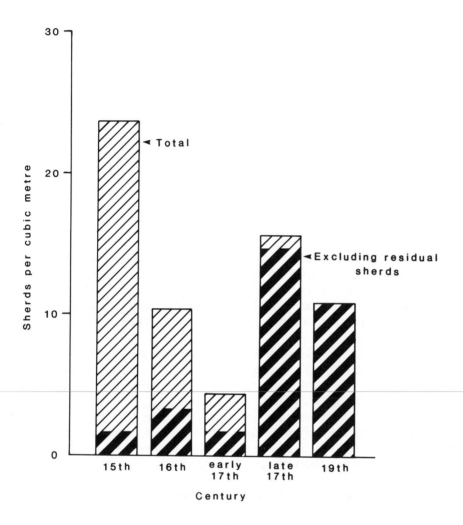

Figure 2.1 Quantity of pottery per unit-volume excavated at Bath Orange Grove. For data see Table 2.1.

The second set of data derives from the author's excavations at Cowdery's Down, where a limited amount of information concerning the excavated volumes could be calculated (Millett, 1984). Information for both sherd numbers and weights, as well as number of bone fragments, were available. The results are shown in Table 2.2 and Figures 2.2–2.4.

Both sets of figures confirm that there are very marked temporal variations. Both illustrate a general increase of material through time (even when we exclude the residual material), and Cowdery's Down shows wide fluctuations from period to period. Because the Bath data represent an aggregate of accumulated urban refuse it can perhaps be taken to give a rough indication of the amount of pottery available through time. The same probably cannot be said of Cowdery's Down where variable intensity of activity and the variable nature of the

Table 2.2: Data from Cowdery's Down (from Millett 1984).

Period	Date range	Estimated excavated volume (m³)	Kg. pottery per m³	potsherds per m³	bone fragments per m³	average sherd weight (g)	Comparative intensity of activity	Types of context represented
1	Early-mid Bronze Age	69.74	0.14	8.8	3.87	15	-	Burial only
2A	Late Bronze Age	5.5	0.0	0.0	2.0	-	same	Construction only
2B	Late Bronze-early Iron Age	10.55	1.72	163.98	19.8	10	increased	Rubbish only
3A	Late Iron Age	3.37	3.04	150.56	79.41	20	same	Rubbish only
3B	Romano-British	40.41	1.02	74.90	22.25	14	decreased	Rubbish only
4C	Anglo-Saxon	55.41	0.003	0.99	0.004	3	increased	Construction and rubbish
5	Post-medieval	8.9	0.4	not available	29.10	not available	decreased	Rubbish only

contexts is extremely important (Table 2.2). It is clear from this table that functional specialisation between periods is extremely influential with burial deposits (Period 1) producing radically different assemblages from rubbish deposits (Periods 2B–3A/B) and constructional features (Periods 2A and the major part of 4C). This is a pattern that we would expect to be common, and illustrates the need for both more data and care in the use of results. One should preferably use aggregate figures from a balanced variety of context types, as comparison of field survey data with such would be particularly appropriate because of the aggregate nature of assemblages from survey. It should incidentally be noted that for survey data, weight represents a better measure of quantity than sherd number because of variations in the friability of the pottery (Table 2.2).

The bone evidence from Cowdery's Down is presented to demonstrate that this also varies from context to context (Fig. 2.4) but does not necessarily behave in the same way as the pottery. Bone cannot thus be used to calibrate variations in the intensity of use of pottery as Alan Vince has suggested (Vince 1977: 72).

Dave Crowther (1983) has recently investigated some post-depositional factors, and has clearly demonstrated how robusticity influences the preservation of the pottery. It does however seem probable that the bias resulting from this will be systematic, and in favour of more advanced technologies. This is perhaps supported by the Cowdery's Down data (Fig. 2.3) which shows that pottery was *more* common in excavated contexts of Periods 2B and 3A (late bronze/late iron age) than in Periods 3B or 5 (Roman and post-medieval). This is partly a function of the change in nature of the site between these periods but is particularly salutory when one knows that the only pottery recovered from the topsoil was Roman and post-medieval.

The application of these results is problematical. Until we have a range of calibration data available it would be a mistake to use them widely or uncritically, especially outside their geographical context. Nevertheless as a purely speculative exercise it is perhaps worth considering the preliminary results of Shennan's East Hampshire Survey (Shennan, 1981), where the number of findspots of Saxon material is six, compared with eighty-six of the Roman period. It is intuitively obvious, given the Cowdery's Down data, that these figures underestimate the intensity of Saxon occupation on the landscape, because their artefacts are more scarce and less robust than those of the Romano-British period. It does not, however, seem reasonable to adjust the figures to correct this bias simply by multiplying the number of Saxon findspots by a factor derived from excavation, for the ratio of Romano-British to Saxon sites need not be the same as the ratio of sherds. What we need to do is to establish a table of equivalence to estimate the "value" of each sherd found. This needs to take into account both the ratio of materials in excavated features, and their relative robustness. Using the Cowdery's Down data, for the former we could suggest that, in the East Hampshire Survey, each individual Saxon sherd should be treated as equivalent in importance to each Roman findspot where more than 75 sherds occur. Their data are as yet unavailable for Shennan's survey but in this way comparisons could be made by scaling down the value of the material from more prolific periods, rather than the more risky method of scaling-up the less visible.

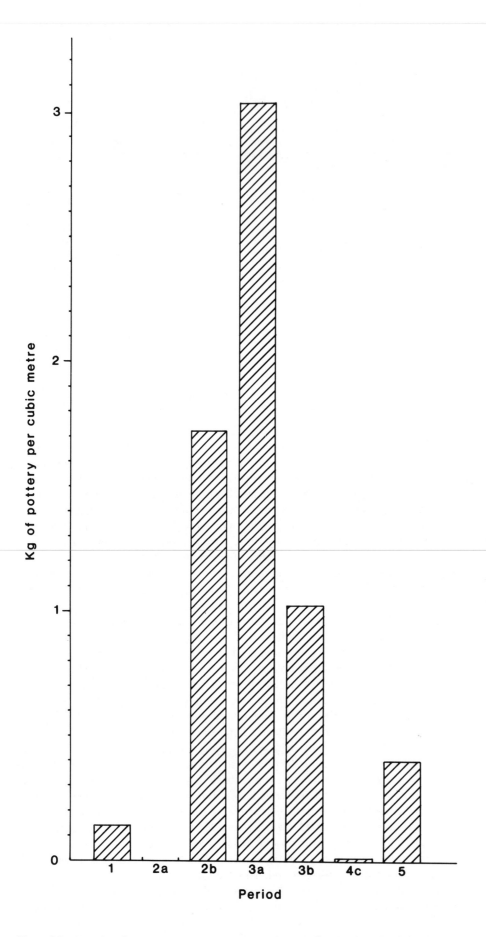

Figure 2.2 Quantity of pottery per unit-volume excavated at Cowdery's Down (by sherd number). For data, see Table 2.2.

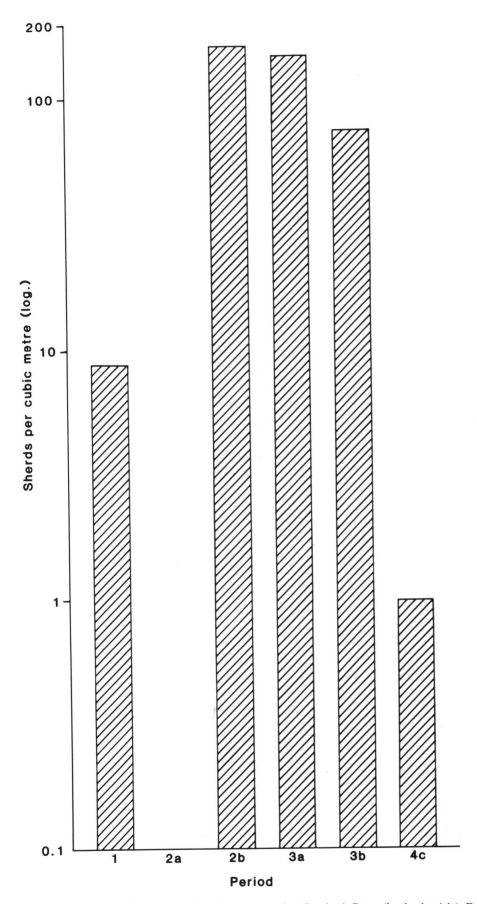

Figure 2.3   Quantity of pottery per unit-volume excavated at Cowdery's Down (by sherd weight). For data, see Table 2.2.

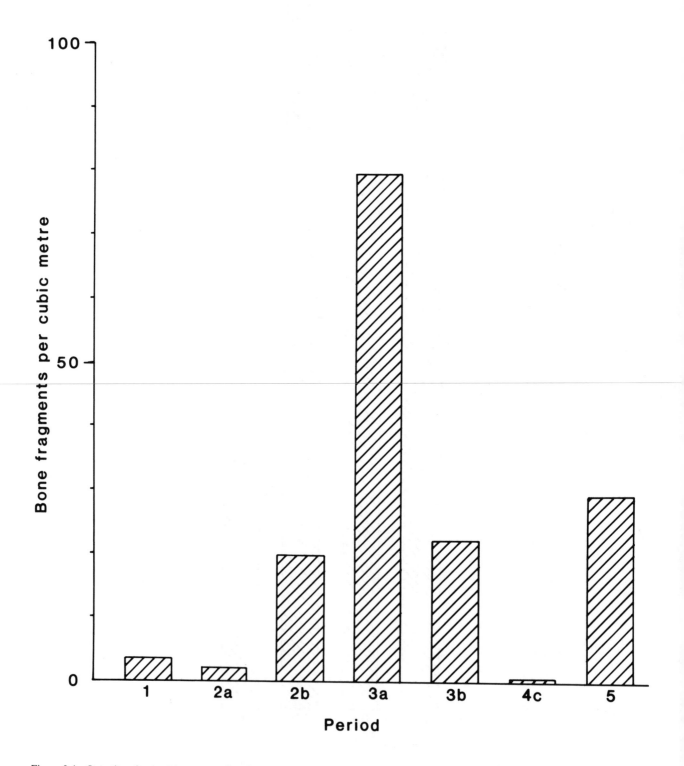

Figure 2.4   Quantity of animal bone per unit-volume excavated at Cowdery's Down. For data, see Table 2.2.

These results are preliminary, and designed only to demonstrate the necessity for calibration. Before more progress can be made, we must

(a) develop better presentation of the results of survey such that quantified data (sherd weight and count) are presented for each findspot.

(b) collect more data from excavation on the quantity of material per-unit-volume from both surface contexts and buried features so that both the quantity of material in circulation, and relative robustness can be established for different spatial and temporal contexts.

Given these data we ought to be able to understand survey data better, and thereby revolutionise our understanding of landscape archaeology.

Acknowledgements

I am most grateful to Dave Crowther, Colin Haselgrove and Tim Schadla-Hall for commenting on a draft of this paper, and restraining me from even greater excesses.

Since the volume went to press, the final report on Stephen Shennan's (1985) East Hampshire Survey, in which many of these problems were made the subject of detailed investigation, has now been published, and ought to be consulted by anyone concerned with the theory and practice of field survey.

Bibliography

Crowther, D.R. 1983 Old land surfaces and modern ploughsoil: implications of recent work at Maxey. *Scottish Archaeological Review* 2/1: 31–44

Millett, M. 1984 Excavations at Cowdery's Down, Basingstoke 1978–81. *Archaeological Journal* 140: 151–279.

O'Leary, T. Forthcoming *Excavations at Bath Orange Grove* (Western Archaeological Trust Monograph)

Shennan, S.J. 1981 Settlement history in East Hampshire. In *The Archaeology of Hampshire*. S.J. Shennan and R.T. Schadla-Hall (eds.) *Hampshire Field Club Monograph* 1: 106–121

Shennan, S.J. 1985 *Experiments in the Collection and Analysis of Archaeological Survey Data: The East Hampshire Survey*. Sheffield: Department of Archaeology and Prehistory

Vince, A.G. 1977 Some Aspects of Pottery Quantification. *Medieval Ceramics* 1: 63–74

3. Sample Bias, Regional Analysis and Fieldwalking in British Archaeology

by Nigel Mills

Introduction

Many of the issues raised in this paper are not new in conception, and have been considered recently in publications by Cherry *et al.* (1978), Groube and Bowden (1982), Loughlin and Miller (1982), Richards (1978), Shennan (1980; 1985) and Thomas (1983) amongst others. My aim is not to provide a comprehensive review of these issues, or of existing archaeological data bases in Britain. Instead, and in line with the brief of the Theoretical Archaeology Group conference in Durham at which a version of this paper was presented, it is hoped to stimulate further discussion by briefly considering a few important themes.

My first objective is to emphasise the fundamental biases and inadequacies contained in existing samples of the spatial distributions of different types of archaeological evidence at the regional scale in Britain. While the archaeological record is inherently biased towards certain types of material remains, the situation has been complicated by selective collection of certain types and classes of evidence, particularly upstanding monuments and cropmark features. Because of their nature, and the techniques used to detect them, these remains tend to occur in particular types of landscape. These include areas of longstanding pasture, especially over higher ground, and areas in which the subsoil favours the creation of crop marks such as gravel terraces and the chalklands. In consequence, existing archaeological data bases tend not to be representative of the full range of evidence for past human activities across the different landscapes that exist within different British regions. The most crucial problem that arises from these biases is that, after over one hundred years of professional research, for most periods we still have little understanding of fundamental questions concerning regional patterns of settlement and land-use. This is despite the fact that, although only one stage in studying the nature and development of prehistoric societies, information concerning the settlement and subsistence system is fundamental to most other aspects of research.

The second aim is to emphasise that regionally based, ecologically stratified, multi-stage data collection programmes (Binford, 1964; Cherry and Shennan, 1978) are the best means of redressing these biases, and ensuring that we obtain adequate samples of the full range of Britain's archaeological heritage to serve for planning, educational and research purposes. Such data collection programmes, involving an integrated range of surface survey techniques (fieldwalking, survey of upstanding remains, aerial photography etc.) should be a primary concern of all archaeological groups whether local or national government, university or otherwise based. This is because such programmes provide the only sound footing for the national and regional data bases on which strategies for excavation, conservation and amenity use may be developed in the light of research, education and planning policies. A conscious, regionally based approach is required since data collection must be structured. A representative sample of evidence will not somehow materialise of its own accord in response to chance events, as there will be in-built biases towards certain types of evidence or area (for instance, areas affected by urban renewal or gravel extraction, or which are known to possess abundant archaeological remains which are under threat).

Although not determining, the natural environment has always had a limiting and directional influence on the spatial distribution and development of human societies through variation in the distribution of natural resources. Prior to the industrial revolution, the spatial distribution of subsistence resources has been the major limiting factor affecting broad patterns of settlement distribution at different periods. Imbalances in the distribution of these resources have ensured that settlement distribution has not been uniform, and that dependent or symbiotic relationships have developed between adjacent but contrasting landscape zones. A regionally based approach, which explicitly takes into account such possible variability and interdependence, is therefore the best means of ensuring that differences in spatial distributions between contrasting landscape zones may be recognised and understood.

Within the regional approach to archaeological data collection, this paper concentrates on fieldwalking techniques designed to obtain information concerning the spatial distribution of artefacts in the plough zone. This emphasis has been chosen since present data bases tend to be biased towards upstanding remains and cropmark features, and hence towards the particular landscape zones which favour the recognition of such evidence. Yet on theoretical grounds, and in the light of empirical evidence produced by recent regionally based fieldwalking programmes in continental Europe, landscape zones with a long history of arable farming may arguably be those in which settlement and land-use have tended to concentrate, at least from the advent of societies based largely on plant husbandry. Upstanding remains are rarely preserved in such areas, where the subsoils are often also unsuitable for the creation of cropmarks. Archaeological evidence for the use of such areas may now only be recoverable through systematic collection of surface artefacts.

It might be argued that such remains are so poorly preserved that they are not worth collecting given the stringent financial limits on archaeological field work, and the need to study existing sites which are under threat. Such an argument is dubious from the points of view both of cultural resource management and of academic research since these remains are of crucial importance in allowing other, better preserved remains to be understood and interpreted to academics and to the public. Recent work (e.g. Bell, 1983; Hayes, in press; Mills, in press a; Smith, 1984) also suggests that even in areas in which the archaeological record has been severely damaged by agriculture and by soil erosion, colluvial processes will often have led to the preservation of significant samples of evidence. Given their importance, the recognition of such circumstances should also be given a high priority, the analysis and understanding of geomorphological processes influencing the archaeological record forming an integral part of field survey design and execution.

Fieldwalking techniques also require emphasis since primary data collection is heavily dominated by excavation, and to a lesser extent by aerial photography and survey of upstanding monuments. The dominance of excavation in field training is seen in most university courses and local government and unit archaeological organisations. Yet fieldwalking requires a high level of specialised competence of a different but complementary nature to that required by excavation, and for which experience of excavation is an inadequate training. Some of the main requirements of a competent fieldwalker may be summarised as follows:

1. a broadly based appreciation of current knowledge concerning natural and human landscapes, their history and their formation processes. This is essential for the design, implementation and interpretaton of survey programmes, ensuring a general appreciation of the problems involved which may then be applied to particular local or regional circumstances. Particular problems requiring specialist training include human use of landscapes under different settlement and subsistence strategies, in relationship to the varying distribution of natural resources at the regional scale; and geomorphological processes (soil erosion, redeposition etc.) affecting landscape evolution and attrition and survival of archaeological remains.
2. a broad knowledge of artefacts of different periods from the Palaeolithic to the post-medieval; an appreciation of cultural processes leading to their occurrence in the archaeological record (processes of production, use, curation, discard etc.); an understanding of how such artefacts and their distributional patterns may be affected by weathering and mass movement.
3. a knowledge of the range, limitations, and applications of the numerous different fieldwalking techniques available and of sampling theory. As with excavation, a wide range of techniques exist, many of which provide different types of information (e.g. Fasham et al., 1980; Mills, in press b) and should therefore be used flexibly to answer particular problems. There is certainly no single technique that can be regarded as ideal since requirements may vary from the need to plot surface artefacts in meticulous detail over small areas to extensive, rapid surveys of large areas. An appreciation is also required of factors affecting artefact recovery in the field including lighting conditions, state of the ploughsoil and weathering, and team management and experience.

The Problems

Recent fieldwalking projects and reviews of existing data bases in the British Isles and continental Europe indicate major gaps and biases in current knowledge concerning the nature, spatial distribution and density of archaeological remains across the landscape (for instance Cherry *et al.*, 1978; Groube and Bowden, 1982; Howell, 1983; Keller and Rupp, 1983; Kruk, 1980; Loughlin and Miller, 1979; Mills, 1980; 1983; and in press a and b; Richards, 1978). Four main types of bias are indicated in existing British Isles data bases:
1. towards particular classes of evidence (e.g. cropmark features, upstanding monuments)
2. towards sites rather than archaeological landscapes
3. towards particular types of site at different periods (e.g. ceremonial and mortuary monuments for the Neolithic, hill-forts for the Iron Age). Domestic sites in general are poorly known for most areas until the Roman period.
4. towards particular landscape zones within given regions (e.g. chalk uplands, gravel terraces)

These biases result from two main sets of variables: the differential nature and quality of preservation of archaeological remains in different landscapes, and methodologies for data collection. For certain classes and types of evidence, the selective operation of these variables has had a compound effect such that present data bases are incapable of answering some of the most basic questions with which archaeologists should be concerned. Domestic sites are the most obvious example, since most British and continental European data bases cannot provide reasonable information concerning how and where the majority of people at different periods lived.

Thus for the British Neolithic, Dennell (1983) has recently underlined the peculiar nature of the existing data base with its overwhelming emphasis on mortuary and ceremonial monuments, and on environmental evidence. It is sobering to note that these same biases were recognised 80 years ago by Pitt-Rivers, and that little has been done to redress them (Barrett *et al.*, 1984: 203). Yet it is evident that it is impossible to understand the role of such mortuary and ceremonial sites without understanding their broader settlement and land-use contexts at the regional scale. As an example, similar problems of bias are apparent for the Neolithic of Languedoc in south-east France. (Mills, 1980; 1983; in press c). Recent assessment of the regional data base by fieldwalking and by geomorphological analysis has revealed that in some areas mortuary monuments are associated with permanent settlements, in others not. More importantly, mortuary monuments are not preserved in those parts of the landscape which evidence from fieldwalking shows were the most intensively settled from the Neolithic onwards.

In Languedoc, the areas of most intensive settlement are entirely cultivated at present, and have been throughout historical times, forming preferred areas of occupation for agrarian societies. The subsoils of these preferred areas of occupation consist predominantly of soft silt- and clay-rich rocks in contrast to the limestone subsoils of other parts of the region from which archaeological remains are best known. During historical times, these upland limestone areas were used mainly as rough grazing for flocks of sheep and goats, except during phases of population increase and resultant pressure on available arable land over the soft rocks. During these phases of population increase settlement spread onto the marginal arable soils of the limestone uplands, producing discontinuities in the history of settlement in these areas. The fieldwalking and geomorphological evidence indicated that the well preserved neolithic remains over the limestone areas are the product of similar processes, representing particular aspects of the settlement and subsistence system at different phases of the Neolithic. During the middle and later Neolithic these remains consist primarily of mortuary monuments and occupation floors in caves, and seem to be the product of seasonal or periodic use of the limestone areas by human communities centred over the soils of soft rocks. For the Chalcolithic of the late third millennium BC numerous stone built settlements are known from the limestone uplands in addition to the mortuary and cave sites, and there is evidence of a marked increase in the density of settlement over the soft rocks. The chalcolithic settlements of the limestone areas therefore seem to represent a phase of expansion of settlement and land-use onto marginal arable land, similar to the population cycles of the historical period.

To take another example, the majority of existing evidence for the development of British society in the Iron Age comes from hill-forts and cemeteries. Again, it is evident that unless hill-forts can be considered in their regional settlement contexts it is impossible to understand their role and development. For instance, how does the distribution of hill-forts relate to centres of population at regional and national scales? In the areas of their construction, did the majority of the population live in the hill-forts or in domestic settlements around them? Similar problems exist in the Auvergne region of central France, where it was noted that the existing iron age data base consisted mainly of hill top sites in areas of historically marginal arable land (Mills, in press b). The few sites known elsewhere were positioned on marshy soils and had been found only recently as a result of modern drainage projects. Systematic fieldwalking has revealed numerous iron age as well as neolithic and bronze age settlements in other areas currently under the plough and which have been cultivated throughout historical times. It now appears that, as was the case in Languedoc, these other areas have formed the main foci of settlement since the Neolithic.

Almost any regional British data base could be used to illustrate these points, which are made not to belittle the high quality of much existing evidence, but to emphasise that this evidence is selective and unrepresentative of regional patterns of settlement. Groube and Bowden (1982) have argued for settlement pattern survey geared to the identification of neolithic and bronze age domestic sites in Dorset, and Richards (1978) has recommended large scale planned fieldwalking programmes for Berkshire to answer similar problems.

However, while these writers have highlighted some of the problems and the means for their solution, it is possible that they have not identified the appropriate scale of analysis required as a result of the constraints of working within modern administrative units and using these as their points of departure in developing data collection programmes. Thus the two surveys mentioned are concerned with landscapes dominated by chalk subsoils on which the majority of known archaeological remains are concentrated within the respective counties.

It may be that for southern Britain a different scale of analysis is needed to identify the problems and to solve them, research being designed at a regional scale to encompass a wider variety of landscape zones and not constrained by county boundaries. Thus chalk landscapes may not initially have been attractive to prehistoric communities practising plant husbandry, the main centres of settlement being concentrated on different soils well away from the chalk. The search for evidence of extensive settlement of the chalk during the Neolithic and Bronze Age might therefore be futile since the chalklands may have been used primarily for pastoral or other purposes in a similar way to that suggested for the extensive limestone dominated uplands of Languedoc. The chalklands may have formed but a part of much more extensive and complex regional patterns of settlement and land-use.

The County of Humberside is of interest in this respect since these problems are encapsulated at a smaller scale than would be required when considering southern Britain. In addition to the chalklands of the Yorksire Wolds, this county also possesses extensive areas with different subsoils, including the sands of the Vale of York to the west, boulder clays to the east, and alluvial silts and gravels (Loughlin and Miller, 1979). The existing data base contains a high concentration of archaeological evidence over the Wolds including numerous cropmark features and upstanding remains. This wealth of evidence over the Wolds is the product both of early work on standing remains by archaeologists such as Greenwell and Mortimer, carried out prior to the spread of mechanised arable farming, and of intensive aerial surveys over the last fifteen years. The majority of these remains are of iron age and Roman date or later, and include cemeteries, settlements and field systems. In contrast, evidence for neolithic and bronze age occupation consists primarily of barrows and isolated finds. Elsewhere some evidence exists from areas with sand and gravel subsoils where cropmarks show up effectively but where the amount of aerial survey has been limited, while there is little archaeological evidence from the boulder clays. Yet as Loughlin (Loughlin and Miller, 1979: 47) points out "some of the most remarkable small finds of many periods from the county originated from this district" (the boulder clays of Holderness). Loughlin suggests that the limited potential of the boulder clay areas for aerial survey, and lack of systematic fieldwalking, have been important factors resulting in this lack of evidence. Considered on a regional scale, it may be that the Wolds provides a biased and incomplete picture of the development of human societies in the area, the main early foci of settlement being off the Wolds, over the sands and gravels and possibly the boulder clays, with some important evidence perhaps now buried beneath extensive recent deposits of alluvium.

These suggestions have both theoretical and empirical support. From the theoretical viewpoint Sherratt (1980; 1981) has recently argued that early cultivators practised horticulture and would have preferred high groundwater soils occurring in river valleys rather than the lighter but drier soils of the interfluves (or chalklands). Heavy, water retentive soils may well have been preferred by early cultivators, provided that only the upper part of the soil profile was tilled. The chalkland and other interfluve soils may only have been taken up subsequently as extensive plough based cereal cultivation developed, or as population increased and settlement spread.

From the empirical viewpoint, evidence has already been cited above which indicates the gaps in existing data bases, and in particular the likelihood that present data are biased against those areas which may have formed the main foci of settlement from at least neolithic times onwards. Recent palynological evidence (Edwards and Hirons, 1984) for pre-elm decline cereals in widely different parts of Britain tend to confirm that present perceptions of a cautious and limited spread of early cultivators are wrong. Instead, it appears that early cultivators became rapidly, firmly, and widely established over the British Isles. The fact that our archaeological data bases contain scant evidence for this occupation suggests we have been looking in the wrong place and for the wrong kinds of evidence.

The suggestions above are of course hypotheses, but they are of critical importance to understanding both the development of prehistoric societies in Britain, and the broader context of the abundant remains that are already known to exist. However, unless these hypotheses are developed and used in designing data collection programmes, there will be little chance of testing them and of coming to a better understanding of the problems they define. This is because under present threats to the known archaeological heritage the tendency will be to concentrate effort and finance where the archaeology and the known threats are most obvious, thereby compounding the biases that already exist. Even in academic circles, which should be freer from such constraints, this tendency is apparent, with a fixation for studying prehistoric social organisation in relationship to existing data bases which are manifestly incapable of answering the questions asked. Thus recent discussions of the British Neolithic have centred on the possible development of chiefdoms and related ceremonial 'core' areas (Bradley and Hart, 1983; Renfrew, 1973). Bradley and Hart (1983) have recently proposed a research design based explicitly on the assumed importance of such 'core' areas for neolithic settlement. Such an explicit statement is welcomed, but it is made in the absence of any firm data on the distribution of neolithic occupation over the country as a whole, and the question must be asked as to whether in fact these 'core' areas stand out purely as a result of the biases inherent in existing evidence? If the main centres of settlement were elsewhere, then research organised around these 'core' areas will neither help us to understand the broader context of the development of the Neolithic, nor to understand the significance of the ceremonial complexes themselves. Such research will serve mainly to reinforce existing biases and assumptions.

Problem Solving

It is increasingly being realised that planned fieldwalking surveys involving systematic collection of surface artefacts can provide some of the answers to the problems outlined above. It is also realised (e.g. Fasham et al., 1980; Richards, 1978) that fieldwalking is an archaeological technique that requires its own training programmes and qualified personnel, and that close attention must be paid to post-depositional factors affecting the preservation and recovery of surface artefacts (Bell, 1983; Hayes, in press; Mills, in press a; Smith, 1984). Several major fieldwalking projects are in progress, including the Fenland Survey organised by the Fenland Survey Co-ordinating Committee and the Stonehenge Environs Project organised by the Trust for Wessex Archaeology.

However, it is suggested here that many of these problems require more broadly based approaches to solve them, transcending where necessary the artificially imposed spatial limits of modern administrative counties. In particular, it is argued that regionally based approaches and flexible aims and methods of data collection should be used. As Groube and Bowden (1982) point out, many of the problems are common to several counties and much effort and financial resources could be wasted by needless duplication of data collection programmes.

A more broadly based, regional approach, integrating contrasting landscape zones (e.g. chalklands, alluvial sands and gravels, boulder clays etc.) seems most appropriate for establishing archaeological data bases since human settlement and subsistence systems have at all periods been conditioned by the differential distribution of natural resources. The development of settlement and land-use in adjacent but contrasting landscape zones tends to be closely tied since imbalances in resource distribution ensure that dependent relationships develop although these will change through time (see for instance Mills, in press b and c). The study of these changing interrelationships forms an important guide to more general processes of societal development. The interrelationship between areas of marginal and preferred arable land is one obvious example of such ties, and was illustrated above for Languedoc in south-east France. In this case, it would have been impossible to understand the significance of late third millennium BC settlement over the limestone uplands without knowledge of settlement development during the Neolithic over adjacent areas with soft rock subsoils.

The first step in designing a programme of archaeological data collection, and/or in assessing the adequacy of existing data bases should therefore consist in defining an appropriate region, and breaking this down into component zones based on geology, pedology, topography etc. which offer different opportunities for settlement and land-use. There are obvious problems of scale here, since the definition of an appropriate region will vary according to the questions being asked. However, this problem of spatial definition ultimately depends on theoretical issues, requiring explicit behavioural models for the ways in which adjacent but contrasting landscape zones may have been integrated under different settlement and land-use strategies. In the case of societies based on crop cultivation, the organisation and development of historical, particularly Medieval, patterns of settlement and land-use across the landscape may provide a useful point of departure.

This approach proved useful in designing research in south-east and central France (Mills, 1980; 1983; in press, b and c) while Howell (1983) and Kruk (1980) have used approaches which are essentially similar in the way they have divided the landscape into different landscape zones, offering contrasting potential for human settlement and land-use.

In areas such as Britain which have been the subject of archaeological enquiry over long periods, the existing data base should then be plotted against the major landscape divisions of the region. In most cases this procedure will reveal biases similar to those noted by Groube and Bowden (1982), Loughlin and Miller (1979), or Richards (1978). Recurring patterns include barrows, hill-forts, and other upstanding remains restricted to areas of upland, and iron age and Roman settlements concentrated over gravel terraces although perhaps also extending onto the uplands, with vast areas of currently arable soils for which little is known apart from isolated finds.

The structure of this existing data base could then be used to designate areas in which data collection programmes need to be concentrated. While the threat to known remains on the chalklands, gravels, etc. is very real, it is argued here that in many cases the most urgent need will be for systematic fieldwalking programmes in areas in which archaeological evidence is presently sparse, where aerial survey produces unsatisfactory results, but which are known to have formed major foci of agrarian settlement from at least the medieval period onwards.

Obviously it would be impossible to attempt to survey a whole region at an adequate level of intensity by fieldwalking. A sampling design will therefore be required from the outset, aimed initially at assessing the quality of existing data in different parts of the region. Whether purposive or probabilistic sampling procedures (Cherry and Shennan, 1978) are used is to some extent irrelevant, the important requirement being that an explicit sampling procedure is adopted, selecting a series of areas for study that will provide a representative cross-section of the different landscape zones. The proportion of each zone studied will obviously depend on the resources and manpower available, but it is important that an overall picture be established as soon as possible (see following).

The delimitation of the units to be covered also requires careful thought, particularly as modern administrative units may be inappropriate. Thus parish boundaries have often been used to delimit survey units, but since these relate to particular types of human landscape imposed in historical times they may not form appropriate units for looking at prehistoric or Roman settlement systems which were not subject to the same economic, social or political controls. The important question is whether the areas defined by parish boundaries provide satisfactory samples of the ecological diversity of the area in question. A more appropriate way of dividing up the landscape might be through the use of the Ordnance Survey grid. For instance, ten kilometre squares might be used to define sample areas of different landscape zones, within which groups of fields might serve as the actual units of study, selecting a 15%–25% sample of each square for fieldwalking.

The data collection and recording techniques must also vary according to the resources available (manpower, finances, time etc.) and the objectives of the survey. A wide range of data collection techniques is now available, and concern has been expressed at this. In particular, some have called for standardisation of collection strategies to enable comparability of results between areas. A degree of standardisation is certainly desirable for observations of field conditions which may affect artefact recovery. For instance, soil types, slope, soil and artefact visibility, weathering etc. are all variables which should be recorded and standards should be agreed for these. Similarly, it would help amateur and other similar groups if a limited range of standardised techniques could be agreed upon to fit different circumstances and objectives. To some extent this has been done in the booklet on survey methods written by Fasham et al., (1980). However, the booklet gives inadequate discussion of which techniques are appropriate for different problems and does not cover the full range of techniques that are available. Beyond these points, any appeal for standardisation fails to recognise that different techniques are designed to produce different types of information to answer different questions. A particular technique will not be able to answer certain questions as well as others, at least within the limits of time, labour, and finance available. There is no single technique which can be considered ideal, providing a happy compromise between speed of work and intensity of data collection. This point serves to emphasise the importance of having clearly specified goals expressed in terms of archaeological problems to be tackled when designing any survey programme, so that appropriate field collection techniques are used.

Towards one end of the range of techniques available, there are extremely detailed, often site specific, methods of data collection which may require the locations of individual artefacts to be recorded to within a few centimetres. Such detailed recording is of importance for analysing variables or processes such as downslope movement of artefacts across a field, weathering patterns, and/or the relationship of surface artefacts to subsurface features. Such techniques are time consuming, requiring in excess of 100 man-hours per 10 hectares where moderate levels of artefact density are present. Thus while providing high quality data about a small area, it would take decades to cover the sorts of area with which most County or other regionally based archaeological groups are concerned, even with a sampling programme. Yet it is important that selective parts of a survey area should be studied in such detail to answer specific questions. These techniques might be appropriate in the second or third stages of a survey programme, in which the earlier stages have produced a picture of varying densities and types of artefact distributions over an area, but where the more detailed information is required to answer specific problems.

In the middle of the range comes a variety of techniques involving recording of artefacts on a grid or line basis, with varying mesh sizes and/or line and collection intervals. The sampling unit is often a field, within which fairly detailed questions may be asked about the distribution of artefacts. The accuracy of recording the spatial locations of artefacts varies from within a metre or so to within a few tens of metres. The time involved also varies according to the mesh size and/or the line and collection interval. Fasham *et al.* (1980) give a range of 10–100 man-hours dependent on the technique being used. These techniques are useful for looking at local variations in artefact type and density, and for defining the limits of scatters or concentrations. They are the most widely used at present, yet it would be wrong to consider them as ideal since when compared with the surface areas which have to be dealt with, and the resources available, they seem to be time consuming. For instance, a ten per cent sample of the ploughed land of Nottinghamshire would require over 30,000 man-hours to complete using a technique that permitted a work rate of 20 man-hours per ten hectares. In other words it would take a full time team of eight people six years to complete, assuming that fields were available for walking for about half a year. The question must therefore be asked as to whether the levels of detail in recording of artefact locations provided by these techniques are strictly necessary. In particular, faced with current threats to our archaeological heritage, and our lack of information concerning the archaeology of ploughed land, we must ask whether more rapid but less detailed techniques might provide the basic information required for initial assessment of the archaeological potential of ploughed areas, for academic and for more general planning purposes.

These more rapid techniques lie at the other end of the range, and are designed to maximise the return of information of particular types from large areas as rapidly as possible. By large areas is meant several hundred square kilometres, and by rapidly is meant within a few months. These are often the sorts of parameters within which public funded archaeological organisations have to operate, yet such rapid spatially extensive surveys are little used in Britain despite their demonstrable cost and quality effectiveness when used as part of regionally based survey programmes in other parts of Europe. This under use seems due to a suspicion that any artefact collection technique that does not involve tight control over spatial locations of artefacts is somehow professionally dubious, and a belief that large, spatially contiguous areas must be surveyed to produce satisfactory data samples. The suspicions and beliefs merely reveal a lack of professionalism, including ignorance both of theoretical and methodological principles involved, and of the practical needs of many County Councils and other organisations for rapid returns of information for investment.

Foley (1981) has recently described techniques for looking at trends in low density artefact scatters across large areas using a point sampling technique. Here the emphasis is placed on related techniques concerned more with identifying artefact clusters (settlement sites, activity areas etc.), although also permitting general trends in artefact variability to be established. Large quadrats (e.g. 500 metre squares) provide the sampling units, within which the minimal recording units might cover several hectares (a field or part of a field for instance). Concentrations of artefacts within each recording unit are bagged separately, and their approximate extent defined, but otherwise all artefacts from a particular unit are bagged together. These techniques permit a work rate of 6 man-hours or less per 10 hectares, although they may require a relatively high proportion of experienced:inexperienced labour (e.g. a minimum of one experienced to three inexperienced workers is desirable).

These techniques have been used successfully in surveys in central France in areas which have similar environmental and land-use characteristics to parts of the British Isles (Mills, in press b). In one case, a twenty per cent sample of an area of 260 km² required the equivalent in man-hours of five to six months work by a team of four, comprising two experienced workers and two trainees. This survey produced over 100 new concentrations of prehistoric and Roman artefacts, mostly pottery. The majority of these concentrations appear to be settlements on the basis of subsequent test excavation or on other grounds. Most of these concentrations were located in ploughed areas previously thought to contain little of archaeological interest prior to the Middle Ages. These results have important implications not only in academic terms, but also for planning and development control. Apart from the recognition of concentrations, it was also possible to observe trends in artefact distributions over different parts of the landscape in question by comparing artefact densities between quadrats or fields.

Of course it is not claimed that such rapid techniques provide a complete picture. Effectively they provide initial glimpses of underlying patterns or trends which may form the basis for future work in an academic context, and/or provide a firm framework for the planning and development control functions of public archaeological organisations. They do have the massive advantage of allowing large amounts of useful information to be collected in short periods of time.

Conclusions

As stated at the beginning of this paper, the aim has not been to provide a comprehensive review of recent discussion of survey techniques, methodologies and theoretical background. The aim has rather been to introduce and briefly develop a few themes which the writer feels are of crucial importance if we are ever to obtain an understanding of the full range and distribution of archaeological evidence for the development of prehistoric societies in Britain. It is argued that the most urgent need is for the implementation of regionally based data collection programmes, whose designs are problem orientated and solidly grounded in explicit theoretical positions. Emphasis should be placed on those landscape zones which are currently least well known archaeologically, but which on theoretical grounds might be expected to have been important settlement centres. Multi-stage strategies will be desirable in most cases, beginning initially with the rapid, spatially extensive techniques outlined above, followed up by more labour intensive techniques where these are needed to answer particular questions. Of necessity such an approach will require considerably more emphasis on fieldwalking and the development of appropriate training programmes. The use of particular methods of artefact collection requires knowledge and awareness of the purposes for which those methods are best suited. This in turn requires awareness of the theoretical and methodological issues, in addition to practical constraints of manpower, finance, etc. Far greater collaboration between universities and local and national archaeological groups will be needed than is currently the case, in order to ensure that adequate numbers of trained personnel are available. The universities in particular have an important role to play in training, and in developing their own regional survey programmes.

Acknowledgements

Thanks are due to Mark Maltby and to Martin Millett who commented on an earlier draft of this paper, and to Pete Hayes for much useful and stimulating discussion. The faults are all my own.

Bibliography

Barrett, J., Bradley, R., Bowden, M. and Mead, B. 1984 South Lodge after Pitt-Rivers. *Antiquity* 57: 193–204

Bell, M. 1983 Valley sediments as evidence of prehistoric land-use on the South Downs. *Proceedings of the Prehistoric Society* 49: 119–150

Binford, L.R. 1964 A consideration of archaeological research design. *American Antiquity* 29: 425–441

Bradley, R. and Hart, C. 1983 Prehistoric settlement in the Peak District during the third and second millennia b.c.: a preliminary analysis in the light of recent fieldwork. *Proceedings of the Prehistoric Society* 49: 177–193

Cherry, J.F. and Shennan, S. 1978 Sampling cultural systems: some perspectives on the application of probabilistic regional survey in Britain. In *Sampling in Contemporary British Archaeology*, J.F. Cherry, C. Gamble and S. Shennan (eds.) pp.17–48 Oxford: British Archaeological Reports, British Series 50

Cherry, J.F., Gamble, C., and Shennan, S. (eds.) 1978 *Sampling in Contemporary British Archaeology*. Oxford: British Archaeological Reports, British Series 50

Dennell, R. 1983 *European Economic Prehistory—a New Approach*. New York: Academic Press.

Edwards, K.J. and Hirons, K.R. 1984 Cereal pollen grains in pre-elm decline deposits: implications for the earliest agriculture in Britain and Ireland. *Journal of Archaeological Science* 11 (1): 71–80

Fasham, P.J., Schadla-Hall, R.T., Shennan, S.J., and Bates, P.J. 1980 *Fieldwalking for Archaeologists*. Winchester: Hampshire Field Club and Archaeology Society

Foley, R. 1981 A model of regional archaeological structure. *Proceedings of the Prehistoric Society* 47: 1-17.

Groube, L.M. and Bowden, M.C.B. 1982 *The Archaeology of Rural Dorset—Past, Present, and Future* (edited by R. Bradley). Dorchester: Dorset Archaeological Committee (Dorset Natural History and Archaeological Society, Monograph 4)

Hayes, P. (in press) Fen edge sediments, stratigraphy and archaeology near Billingsborough, south Lincolnshire. In *Paleoenvironmental Investigations*, D. Gilbertson, N. Fieller and N.G.A Ralph (eds.) Oxford: British Archaeological Reports

Howell, J. 1983 *Settlement and Economy in Neolithic Northern France*. Oxford: British Archaeological Reports, International Series 157

Keller, D.R. and Rupp, D.W. (eds.) 1983 *Archaeological Survey in the Mediterranean Area*. Oxford: British Archaeological Reports, International Series 155

Kruk, J. 1980 *The Neolithic Settlement of Southern Poland*. Oxford: British Archaeological Reports, International Series 93

Loughlin, N. and Miller, K.R. 1979 *A Survey of Archaeological Sites in Humberside*. Hull: Humberside Joint Archaeological Committee/Humberside Libraries and Amenities Department

Mills, N.T.W. 1980 *Prehistoric Agriculture in Southern France—Case Studies from Provence and Languedoc*. Unpublished PhD dissertation, Sheffield University

Mills, N.T.W. 1983 The neolithic of southern France. In *Ancient France* C. Scarre (ed.) pp.91–145. Edinburgh: Edinburgh University Press

Mills N.T.W. (in press a) Geomorphology and settlement archaeology. In *Palaeoenvironmental Investigations*, D. Gilbertson, N. Fieller and N.G.A. Ralph (eds.) Oxford: British Archaeological Reports

Mills, N.T.W. (in press b) Iron Age settlement and society in Europe— contributions from field surveys in central France. In *Archaeological Field Survey in Britain and Abroad* S. Macready and F.H. Thompson (eds.) pp.74–100. London: Society of Antiquaries (Occasional Papers No. 6)

Mills N.T.W. (in press c) Regional survey and settlement trends: studies from prehistoric France. In *Beyond Domestication*, G.W.W. Barker and C. Gamble (eds.) pp.181–203. New York: Academic Press

Renfrew, C. 1973 *Before Civilisation.* London: Jonathan Cape

Richards, J. 1978 *The Archaeology of the Berkshire Downs: an Introductory Survey.* Reading: Berkshire Archaeological Committee Publications, 3

Shennan, S. 1980 Meeting the plough damage problem: a sampling approach to area intensive fieldwork. In *The Past Under the Plough*, J. Hinchliffe and R.T. Schadla-Hall (eds.) pp.125–33. London: Department of the Environment

Shennan, S. 1985 *Experiments in the Collection and Analysis of Archaeological Survey Data: The East Hampshire Survey.* Sheffield: Department of Archaeology and Prehistory, University of Sheffield

Sherratt, A.G. 1980 Water, soil and seasonality in early cereal cultivation. *World Archaeology* 11 (3): 313–330

Sherratt, A.G. 1981 Plough and pastoralism: aspects of the secondary products revolution. In *Pattern of the Past*, I. Hodder, G. Isaac and N. Hammond (eds.) pp.261–305. Cambridge: Cambridge University Press

Smith, R.W. 1984 The ecology of neolithic farming systems as exemplified by the Avebury region of Wiltshire. *Proceedings of the Prehistoric Society* 50: 99–120

Thomas, C. (ed.) 1983 *Research Objectives in British Archaeology.* London: Council for British Archaeology

PART 2

CASE STUDIES

4. Identifying Neolithic Settlements in Britain: the Role of Field Survey in the Interpretation of Lithic Scatters

by Robin Holgate

"The missing settlement data from ... [the neolithic] period and in the succeeding earlier Bronze Age is the largest area of 'blindness' in British prehistory and demands the most urgent concentration of effort" (Groube and Bowden, 1982: 31).

The neolithic period in Britain is renowned for its paucity of settlement sites. The original character of these sites and their subsequent denudation are two factors which account for this "area of 'blindness'", but our blinkered perception of the nature of these sites has also been a contributory factor. Over much of south-east Britain, denudation has disturbed or destroyed neolithic land surfaces and shallow subsoil contexts such as postholes. Pits and gullies containing domestic debris occasionally come to light by chance, either through the excavation of later period sites (e.g. Bishopstone, Sussex: Bell, 1977) or through quarrying and similar earthmoving activities (e.g. Thrupp, Oxfordshire: Jones *et al.*, 1979). But once the artefacts from these contexts become exposed to natural weathering agencies, those composed of organic and ceramic materials frequently disintegrate. However, lithic artefacts are more resilient and are easily recognisable on the surface of disturbed ground. Since the mid-nineteenth century large collections of flint artefacts, now mostly housed in museums, have been amassed by amateur collectors. Clearly, controlled surface collection survey is the most promising field survey method for retrieving traces of domestic and other activities of neolithic date from areas of disturbance. The aim of this short paper is to discuss the potential and limitations of this form of field survey as a method for locating and defining neolithic settlement sites.

The Nature of Lithic Scatters

The use and discard of lithic artefacts, including both debitage and implements, by past stone-using societies would have taken place across the landscape as a whole (Foley, 1981: 12). A continuous scatter of lithic artefacts, varying in density according to the nature and intensity of land use and the availability of lithic raw materials, would thus be expected to cover those parts of Britain exploited by lithic tool-using populations. Within this diffuse scatter, one would expect to find concentrations of lithic artefacts "which represent acts of discard repeated by numbers of individuals over a span of time. Common knowledge of contemporary human behaviour leads us to expect that many of these concentrated patches of material relics are associated with 'settlement' nodes, but nodes which can be termed quarries, 'factories', butchery locales, etc. may also produce distinctive accumulations" (Isaac, 1980: 133–4).

But how can these concentrated areas of lithic artefacts be identified; and how can they subsequently be interpreted in terms of the human activities which led to their formation?

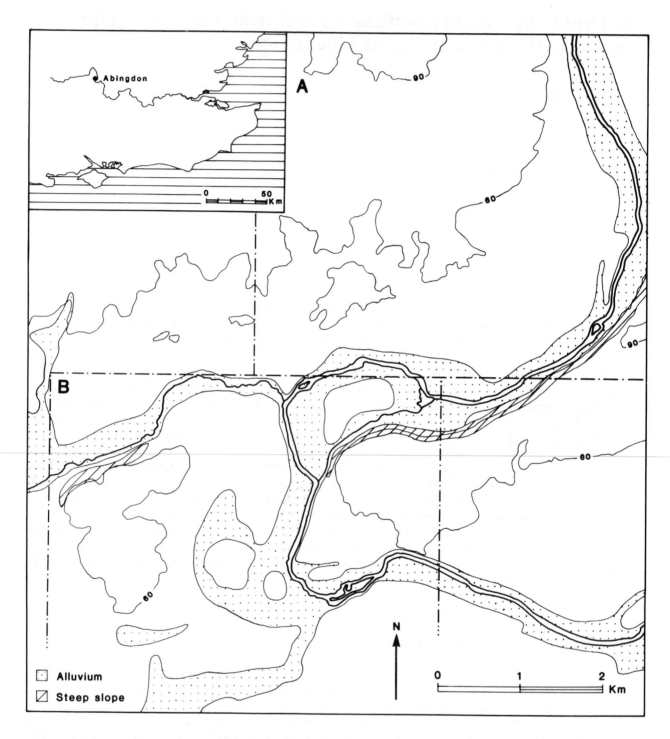

Figure 4.1   The Abingdon area: topography and extent of alluvium. Contours are in metres OD.

The identification of the concentrations is hindered by three main factors. First, zones of greater or lesser lithic artefact density can be created by post-depositional processes acting in the landscape, as demonstrated by the fact that areas of alluvial or colluvial deposits will produce spurious surface scatters of lithic artefacts. Second, land use and availability of lithic raw material vary from region to region, so that the quantity and type of lithic artefacts deposited also vary accordingly. Thus the gravels of the Thames Valley or the clays of the London Basin differ from the chalk Downs in the average density of lithic artefacts encountered per unit area and make comparisons between these regions difficult to calibrate. To give an example of this, the survey of the Thames gravels around Abingdon discussed below produced, on average, a third of the quantity of lithic artefacts per unit area than a corresponding survey conducted by myself and Julian Thomas in Autumn 1983 on the chalk Downs around Avebury. And third, biases in collection, i.e. field and light conditions, length of time spent searching one place, etc., can create artificial concentrations unrelated to past human behaviour. These problems are best overcome by assessing the nature and extent of post-depositional processes acting on the area under study, and then quantifying the thin, continuous 'offsite' scatter of lithic artefacts in this area by an extensive, systematic surface collection survey. Once these factors have been assessed it should be possible to discern concentrations of lithic artefacts, both in terms of numbers and by the presence of specific types of implements or debitage, which represent the loci of past human activity.

The interpretation of these concentrations is nevertheless a far from easy task. Studies of the way in which present-day stone-using societies manufacture, use and discard lithic artefacts provide one line of enquiry, but those carried out to date are largely concerned with hunter-gatherer societies (e.g. Binford, 1978). However, two useful points emerge from a review of the literature currently available on the subject. First, sites witnessing the performance of a range of activities, for example settlement sites, produce a wide variety of artefact-types within the total lithic assemblage (Gould, 1980: 132). Second, use location rarely equals discard location within living areas (Murray, 1980), but discard localities (i.e. middens or refuse pits) are usually discrete and situated close to activity areas (e.g. Clark and Kurashina, 1981: 316–17; David, 1971: 113; Hayden and Cannon, 1983: 128). This suggests that it might be possible to interpret concentrations of lithic artefacts containing a range of different implements and debitage as sites where people lived.

The ideal way to interpret these concentrations, though, is by excavation: either to locate subsoil contexts containing non-lithic artefacts; or to recover further lithic artefacts that will enable a study of the technological and functional aspects of this assemblage to be carried out by refitting debitage and implements, and, in some situations, by the application of micro-wear analysis. This would give an indication of both the range and duration of activities practised on the site, but is expensive in terms of time, labour and finance. Can field survey be used to provide a cheaper and less time-consuming alternative?

The Abingdon Survey: a Case Study (Fig. 4.1)

The Abingdon survey was initiated to find out if discrete concentrations of lithic artefacts which can be interpreted as domestic sites are discernible within the more widespread lithic scatter distributed across the landscape. The area around Abingdon was chosen for three main reasons. First, several large flint scatters and pits containing domestic debris are already known in the area, either as a result of excavation or collection from the surface of ploughed land and areas of gravel extraction (lettered A-G in Fig. 4.2). Otherwise there has not been any significant removal of archaeological material from the ground surface prior to commencing the survey under discussion. Second the landscape consists of flat gravel terraces linked to one another by very gentle slopes. Post-depositional transformations are therefore minimal and restricted to alluviation on the Thames floodplain and possibly slope creep on some of the steeper slopes (see Fig. 4.1). Finally, a large proportion of land in this region is cultivated annually, with almost each successive ploughing biting deeper into the subsoil so that most contexts that once contained flint artefacts (for example middens, original land surfaces and shallow pits) have now become incorporated within the plough soil.

In order to cover as large an area as possible in the time available, in a uniform fashion, a sequential sampling strategy was adopted. Since all the neolithic flint concentrations previously recovered were no less than 100 metres in diameter, it was decided to walk sequential transects at 50 metre intervals across every field under cultivation, bagging the flint artefacts from each 50 metre section separately. The area between each transect was quickly walked to check that artefact scatters less than 50 metres in diameter were not being missed. This exercise was fully justified as in one instance a small scatter of Romano-British pottery and building material, c. 20 metres in diameter, was located. However, no further neolithic flint clusters were recovered. A small team (less than six people at any given time) of experienced field walkers carried out the survey over the winter months of 1982–83. Several fields walked in 1982 were rewalked in late 1983 after the

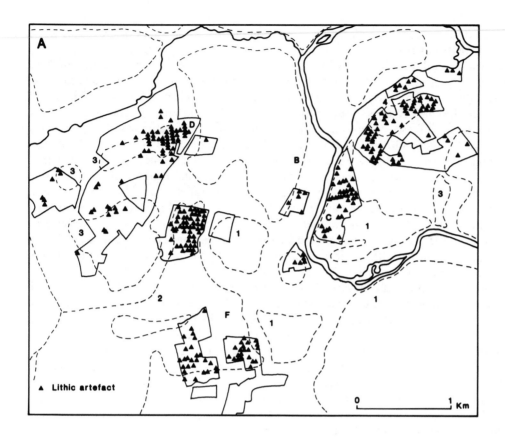

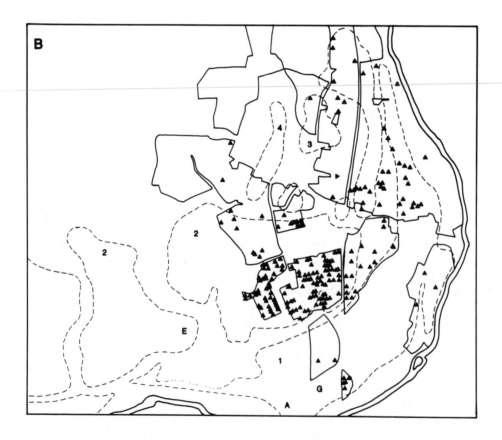

Figure 4.2 The Abingdon survey: distribution of lithic artefacts on cultivated land. The solid lines represent the limit of areas walked. Gravel terraces are indicated by the broken lines and are numbered in sequence. A, E, F & G represent excavated contexts containing domestic debris; B, C & D (as well as A & G) are lithic artefact concentrations located prior to the initiation of the survey described in this paper.

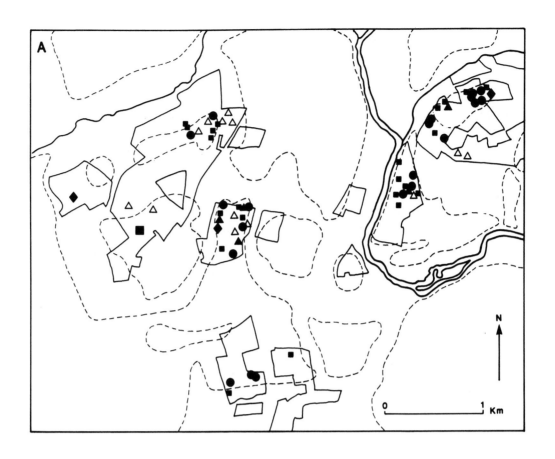

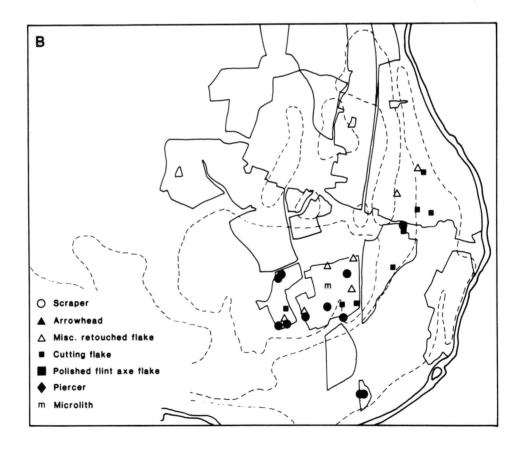

Figure 4.3   The Abingdon survey: distribution of lithic implements on cultivated land.

farming cycle had turned full circle: similar densities and distributions of flint artefacts were recorded in all cases. The results are plotted in Figures 4.2 and 4.3.

Figure 4.2 shows that there is both an almost continuous low density spread of flint artefacts across the landscape and a number of discrete concentrations. Can the concentrations be interpreted as relating to settlement sites? Figure 4.3 shows that these flint concentrations also contain a high proportion and diverse range of implements. In addition, two of these concentrations (letters C and D on Fig. 4.2) had previously been walked by amateur archaeologists, producing large quantities of implements: these included polished flint axe fragments and flakes, arrowheads, scrapers, piercers, notched pieces and knives. Apart from sheer quantity alone, these concentrations can also be distinguished from the surrounding diffuse scatter by the range of implements they contain.

Further information on the nature of two of these concentrations has come to light during the course of recent excavations around Abingdon in advance of gravel extraction and housing development. Excavations at Barton Court Farm (letter E on Fig. 4.2) and Thrupp (A) both produced subsoil contexts containing domestic debris (neolithic pottery, domesticated animal bones, carbonised seeds and charcoal) in association with flint assemblages consisting of a high proportion and wide variety of implements (Miles, 1978; Jones *et al.*, 1979: 8). The nature of archaeological investigations at these sites did not permit a surface collection survey prior to excavation, but in each case large quantities of lithic artefacts were recovered from the topsoil dumps.

Where evidence for domestic activity of neolithic date has been recovered, this has been found in association with both dense surface concentrations of flint artefacts and a flint assemblage containing a large quantity and range of various implements. Is it possible to infer that all surface concentrations with a variety of implements (that cannot be accounted for by collection bias or natural agencies) represent settlement sites? Analogy with the residues of present-day stone-using societies and analysis of the lithic assemblages associated with other traces of domestic activity recovered from neolithic sites in both Britain and Europe (Holgate, in prep.) suggest that this could be the case.

Discussion and Concluding Remarks

The two main questions arising from this survey concern the nature of neolithic settlement sites and the interpretation of surface scatters of flint artefacts that cannot be interpreted as sites of domestic activity. At present, not enough is known about neolithic flint-flaking techniques or the use to which flint artefacts were put during this period, thus making it difficult to reconstruct the activities carried out on sites which only survive as flint scatters. Excavation and subsequent post-excavation analysis of a number of these sites should therefore be undertaken as the first stage in resolving these questions. Information on the activities performed in places where flint artefacts have been manufactured, used and discarded is still contained in the artefacts themselves. By carefully excavating and recovering every artefact in a scatter, and then refitting these pieces to reassemble the original lumps of raw material that were flaked, it is possible to reconstruct not only the core reduction sequences followed in the course of flaking but also the way in which the site was maintained. For example, it should be possible to estimate the length of time the site was in use and, by observing which pieces are either consistently missing or have undergone several stages of modification, to gain an insight into the activities that took place on and off the site. Work of this nature has been undertaken on several palaeolithic and mesolithic flint scatters, both in Britain and elsewhere (e.g. at Hengistbury Head, Dorset: Barton, 1981 and at Pincevent in France: Leroi-Gourhan and Brézillon, 1966), but has yet to be carried out on a neolithic site in Britain.

A programme of excavation to provide further information on the way flint was used in the neolithic period is therefore essential to a fuller understanding of the nature of flint scatter sites. An investigation of this sort need not be restricted to the analysis of *in situ* flaking floors and discard areas. Even for sites where such contexts have become dispersed throughout natural soil horizons (for example at Hengistbury Head, Dorset: Barton, 1981) or where it is only possible in the time available to recover a small proportion of the artefacts on the site (as exemplified by Langweiler 8 on the Aldenhovener Platte, West Germany: de Grooth, 1981; and pers. comm.), refitting has produced information on the structure and maintenance of these sites.

At present, field survey can only put dots on a map or provide information on the degree of preservation of a site. This, in itself, is of value as neolithic settlements are conspicuous by their paucity and any addition in numbers will help give a better picture of the parts of the landscape that were inhabited throughout. In addition, provenancing the lithic raw materials on which artefacts recovered from these sites were manufactured can give some insight into lithic raw material procurement. When the nature of lithic artefact scatters has been investigated further by excavation, it should be possible to determine the activities practiced at a particular site from surface remains alone. Until this work has been done, field survey *per se* is restricted in the role it can play in reconstructing the subsistence strategies and settlement patterns of neolithic populations in Britain.

Acknowledgements

I am indebted to Bill Skellington, Mr. and Mrs. R. Henderson and Jeff Wallis for showing me the flint artefacts in their collections; and to all those, especially Jeff Wallis, Claire Halpin and Roger Ainslie, who helped with the fieldwalking.

Bibliography

Barton, R.N.E. 1981 Some conjoined artefacts from a new Mesolithic site at Hengistbury Head, Dorset. *Proceedings of the Dorset Natural History and Archaeological Society* 103: 13–20

Bell, M. 1977 Excavations at Bishopstone. *Sussex Archaeological Collections* 115.

Binford, L.R. 1978 *Nunamiut Ethnoarchaeology*. New York: Academic Press

Clark, J.D. and Kurashina, H. 1981 A study of the work of a modern tanner in Ethiopia and its relevance for archaeological interpretation. In *Modern Material Culture: The Archaeology of Us*. R.A. Gould and M.B. Schiffer, (eds.) pp.303–321. New York: Academic Press

David, N. 1971 The Fulani Compound and the archaeologist. *World Archaeology* 3: 111–31

Foley, R. 1981 *Off-Site Archaeology and Human Adaptation in Eastern Africa. Cambridge Monographs in African Archaeology* No. 3. British Archaeological Reports, International Series 97

Gould, R.A. 1980 *Living Archaeology*. Cambridge: Cambridge University Press

de Grooth, M.E.Th. 1981 Fitting together Bandkeramik flint. In *Third International Symposium on Flint*, F.H.G. Engelen (ed). Maastricht

Groube, L.M. and Bowden, M.C.B. 1982 *The Archaeology of Rural Dorset: Past, Present and Future*. Dorset Natural History and Archaeological Society. (Monograph 4)

Hayden, B. and Cannon, A. 1983 Where the Garbage Goes: refuse disposal in the Maya Highlands. *Journal of Anthropological Archaeology*. 2 (2): 117–63

Isaac, G. 1980 Stone Age visiting cards: approaches to the study of early land use patterns. In *Pattern of the Past, Studies in Honour of David Clarke*. I. Hodder, G. Isaac, and N. Hammond (eds.) pp.131–55. Cambridge: Cambridge University Press

Jones, G., Wallace, G. and Skellington, W. 1979 Abingdon, Oxfordshire. *CBA Group 9 Newsletter* 9: 8

Leroi-Gourhan, A. and Brézillon, M. 1966 L'habitation Magdalénienne No. 1 de Pincevent, près Monterau (Seine-et-Marne). *Gallia Prehistoire, Fouilles et Monuments Archéologiques en France Métropolitian*, Tome 9, Fasicule 2, 263–385. Paris

Miles, D. 1978 Abingdon/Radley, Barton Court Farm, 1972–6. *CBA Group 9 Newsletter*, 8: 106–7

Murray, P. 1980 Discard location: the ethnographic data. *American Antiquity* 45: 490–502

5. Approaching the Fens the Flexible Way

by David Crowther, Charles French and Francis Pryor

Introduction

With a few notable exceptions (for example, the work of Bulleid and Gray at Glastonbury, Clark at Star Carr; more recently the Somerset Levels Project, and latterly the Fenland Project) dryland archaeology has dominated the discipline in England since its earliest beginnings. Whilst this is hardly to be wondered at, the limitations of such a manifestly weak data set could be said to be severely handicapping modern archaeological theory building. This is particularly true of prehistory, where many of the liveliest theoretical stances currently adopted depend upon the application of analogy; empirical observations from other highly relevant disciplines, such as anthropology or ecology, are used for the elucidation of archaeological evidence, and (ultimately) the explanation of cultural processes. Without criticising such vital work, one can suggest that before scoring any explanatory goals, it is desirable to know the shape and size of the ball. "What is necessary is a reassessment of what archaeological field data represents, i.e. how is the archaeological record formed?" In asking this question, Foley (1981a: 1) like Schiffer before (1976) highlights a crucial issue which archaeologists have long recognised, yet frequently ignored. By grasping this taphonomic nettle of formation and transformation through the explication of predepositional, depositional, and post-depositional processes, one can indeed begin to conceive of an archaeological record as a "palimpsest not dissimilar to minestrone soup" (Gamble, 1982). While highlighting the complexity of the record, such work should remind one also of fundamental weaknesses and biases.

One of the authors has recently argued that the theoretical or explanatory role of archaeology is in danger of becoming a self-perpetuating vortex of academic speculation (Pryor, 1983c). If the blame lies—only in part—with the weakness of conventional evidence, then clearly there is an urgent need within the discipline for new classes of data, rather than simply more of the same. The recent (1983) Spring Conference of the Prehistoric Society gave food for thought. Devoted to "European Wetlands in Prehistory", it served to highlight the remarkable and often unique ranges of evidence recoverable from wetland contexts.

The Fens are the greatest area of wetlands in Britain, and as such offer enormous potential for prehistoric research given that:

a. certain areas have evidence to suggest intensive prehistoric activity shown by numerous discoveries of funerary and communal monuments, or surface finds clusters which comprise a wide variety of fabrics and types.

b. Large tracts of the region were covered in successive deposits of marine (silts) and freshwater bog (peats) formations, variously preserving landscapes of pre-second millennium bc date. Within and below these deposits, archaeological and environmental evidence can be of exceptional quality, due to waterlogging and protection from post-depositional transforms.

c. Modern drainage and cultivation, leading to peat dessication and deflation has led to the exposure of higher parts of undulating buried landscapes. As a consequence, "sites" have been discovered, and thus the archaeological importance of the area has been recognised just in time.

The research potential, and concomitant problems, do not stop for the archaeologist at the western limit of the peat. The complex sequence of marine and freshwater inundations in the region has had severe consequences for the major rivers that drain into the Fen basin. In particular, the impedence of the Welland outfall, coupled with more intensive agriculture upstream, has led, since at least the first millennium bc, to the widespread deposition of alluvium around the western Fen edge and within the valley floor north west of Peterborough. These alluvial spreads have masked, and therefore preserved, much of the riverine and Fen edge landscape that offered such a variety of resources for exploitation in prehistoric times.

As Figure 5.1 shows, alluvium is by no means ubiquitous in the lower Welland Valley. Where alluvial spreads are thin or absent, evidence for human activity over millennia is widespread and widely known, both in the Welland (RCHM, 1960, and Nene Valleys (Pryor, 1974; 1978; 1980a; 1983a). Dense cropmark evidence from the freely draining coarse loams that overlie the terrace gravels include ceremonial, land management and settlement complexes from the Neolithic period onwards. Not surprisingly, this archaeological visibility also includes substantial populations of finds located on, and in, the modern ploughzone. That these areas where alluvium is absent have been subjected to considerable plough damage is not open to question. What may be in doubt is the extent to which modern cultivation has seriously truncated earthfast features in these areas, given that widespread surface collections of artefacts may be derived from the original land surface—an archaeological context that was embraced by the plough at least a thousand years ago (Crowther, 1983).

Such, then, are some of the physiographic variations found within the region under consideration (Fig. 5.1). The region consists of two ecological zones: the lower Welland Valley, and the northwestern part of the Cambridgeshire Peat Fens. To some extent, these zones are methodological, even philosophical constructs; only the "Early Neolith" heavily blessed with the gift of precognition could have drawn quite the dramatic distinction as the modern archaeologist does between areas that only later evolved so differently. The theoretical rationale behind a survey and excavation programme in the lower Welland Valley has been published for some time (Pryor, 1980b) and will not be repeated here. Its extension eastwards into areas below alluvium (Etton Excavations Project) and into the investigations of wider areas below peat and peaty alluvium in the fen-proper (Southwest Fen Project) are logical, indeed essential steps towards elucidating further the adapting, and apparently adaptable, societies that lived in a region that wears environmental determinism as comfortably as a Fen Tiger wears his old wellies.

Scope and content of this paper

This paper sets out neither to "knock" dryland archaeology, nor to "sell" wetland archaeology. There is (or should be) no dichotomy. We hope to show that the one may be used to elucidate the other, that both have assets and liabilities for the study of human development, and that significantly, their respective strengths and weaknesses may be largely mutually exclusive or complementary.

In accordance with the scope and objectives of this volume, particular attention will be paid to archaeological survey; or rather to issues that in the authors' view seem significant in the light of such survey. However, survey without excavation, like excavation without survey, is rarely more than of limited value, and such a division would certainly be unhelpful in the region under consideration here. Evidence from either technique will be presented where appropriate; that from excavation will be used selectively to develop argument which has sprung from some of the survey work accomplished to date.

The paper that follows falls into four sections:
1. The environmental evidence: problems and potential *by Charles French*
2. Exposure and attrition: an example of dryland archaeological visibility from Maxey, in the lower Welland valley *by David Crowther*
3. Exposure and preservation: a few thoughts on surface and subsurface sampling in the Snail valley—some future work? *by David Crowther and Charles French*
4. Fenland dyke survey—its rationale (a question of scale) *by Francis Pryor*

Each of these sections takes a specific issue and examines it in the light of recent fieldwork, using examples or case studies where appropriate.

Any study area that embraces river terraces, Fen margin and Fenland areas, will include a very wide variety of physiography; whatever the merits of goal-oriented, rigidly structured research designs, their implementation in the field—particularly this field—calls for flexibility above all else. This will be apparent in the discussions that follow, in that each of the authors' submissions approach broadly the same problem—the study of prehistoric people in their physical and social environment through time—in rather different ways.

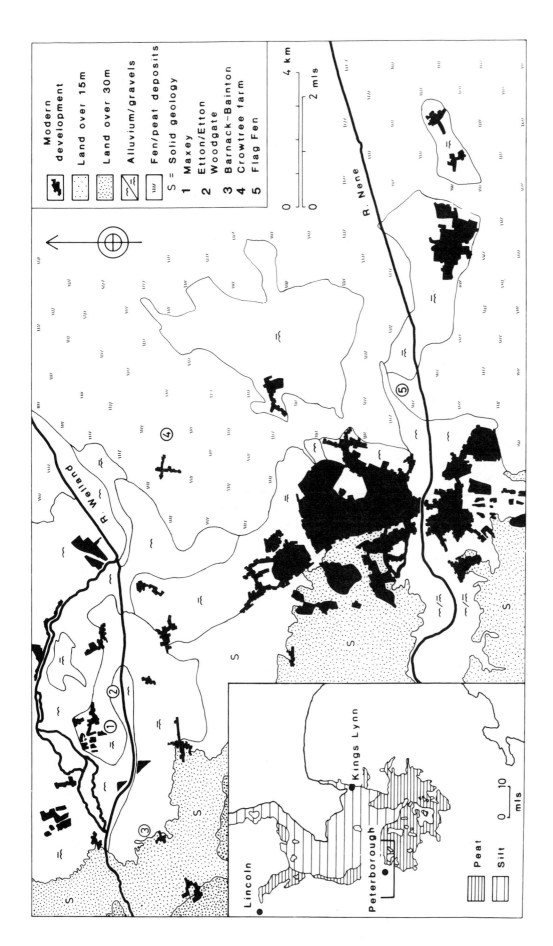

Figure 5.1 The lower Welland and Nene, and their (now canalised) entry into the Fenland. Sites mentioned in the text: (1) Neolithic cursus, henge and mortuary structure complex; (2) Neolithic causewayed enclosure, and (?) partially enclosed settlement; (3) Late neolithic soil profile below medieval headland; (4) Neolithic land surface below Fen deposits; (5) Late bronze age wooden platform below Fen margin/Fen deposits.

61

1. The environmental evidence: problems and potential.

by Charles French

During the past four years of fieldwork in the lower Welland Valley and the adjacent Fen-edge to the north and east of Peterborough, much time and energy has been spent on sampling dry cropmark sites. Now that the analyses of several sites have been completed it is apparent that only limited classes of environmental evidence have been recoverable, but these are nevertheless of considerable importance. As the emphasis of our fieldwork programme has shifted eastwards and Fen-wards, a much greater potential for new, more varied and abundant classes of environmental evidence has become available. These differences in scale and preservation require new avenues of investigative approach.

The following is not intended to provide an exhaustive ecological context for sections 2 and 4, though it does present some of the widespread evidence now available (for a full account, see French 1983). Rather, it highlights, through examples, some of the problems and potential of palaeoenvironmental studies through survey and excavation, in both the lower Welland Valley, and the Fens and Fen margins to the north and east of Peterborough.

Maxey. An example of a dry, exposed, plough damaged site (Fig. 5.1: site 1)

Maxey is a multi-period sequence of "sites" of neolithic to Romano-British periods. Samples were taken for the analysis of soil, phosphate and macro-botanical evidence, as part of the extensive ploughsoil studies undertaken at Maxey. The results were perhaps more pertinent to the archaeology of the site than elucidating the local or regional environment.

Particle size analysis of samples taken from the A- and (where surviving) B-horizons across medieval ridge and furrow suggest that homogenization of soil texture and structure had occurred as a result of ploughing, but was unlikely to have moved artefacts etc. significantly either laterally or vertically. Unlike Taylor's (1979) study of cropmarks and ploughsoil, archaeological features were not discernible in the ploughsoil; the soil and cropmarks appeared to be largely a result of a greater moisture content in the archaeological features, with a slightly greater organic matter content being a contributing factor, rather than differences in soil composition.

Particularly useful results were forthcoming from the ploughsoil phosphate analysis. This suggested areas of possible domestic or animal use which was further amplified by the phosphate sampling of the excavated surface and archaeological features (D.A. Gurney, pers. comm.).

Similar surface- and feature-derived samples for macro-botanical evidence were perhaps less successful. Although indicating that there had been little or no contamination of the archaeological features from modern crops and cropping methods (F. Green, pers. comm.), the evidence obtained was limited due to neutral or slightly alkaline soil conditions. This was compounded by the absence of waterlogging due to recent pumping operations in advance of gravel quarrying. By contrast, Simpson's excavations at Maxey in the early 1960's produced waterlogged organic mud deposits containing a mollusc population (Evans, 1972) far more abundant than anything recovered in the 1979–1981 excavations. This absence of waterlogging with base-rich ground water has resulted in ground conditions being far less calcareous, so that only certain elements of a once rich molluscan fauna has survived. Within two decades, much of the potentially recoverable evidence has been lost.

Highly productive results were forthcoming from the thin sectioning of buried soils, or the micromorphology of palaeosols. Whether by accident or design, a medieval headland was situated above the central mound within the henge, and the mortuary structure located at the henge entrance (see Fig. 5.2). Thin sectioning of the palaeosol beneath the mortuary structure/small ovoid long barrow revealed that a textural B-horizon was all that remained of the former soil profile. The turf and the A-horizon had been removed in antiquity, presumably as a result of the construction of the mortuary structure. This buried B-horizon contained indications that it was once under stable, probably wooded conditions. It then suffered disturbances of some kind, possibly clearance, and later some slight soil disturbance which suggests cultivation or some other activity which reached deep into the soil.

The buried soil beneath the nearby central mound within the henge consisted of a lower A-horizon which remained more-or-less undisturbed by agriculture. Only the upper part of the A-horizon, primarily the turves which were used to construct the first phase of the mound, had been removed in antiquity. This palaeosol had a laminated fabric which suggests a considerable loessic component. Both deforestation and subsequent cultivation elsewhere in the lower Welland Valley may have contributed to the wind-blown component of this pre-late neolithic soil. However, there is also the possibility that some part of the loessic component was inherently present in the subsoil as a result of late Devensian/early Flandrian erosion.

While the above examples may represent good environmental evidence with important implications for former land use, the required preservation is fortuitous and exceptional. Apart from recent work conducted by the author at Barnack/Bainton and elsewhere (French, 1983), the only significant evidence from the last 25 years of (sporadic) archaeological research in the area, comprises two pollen analyses at nearby Tallington. These indicate that the valley floor was probably substantially open by the late Bronze Age (French, 1983) and significantly open by the Roman period (Simpson, 1966: 20).

The palaeo-environmental insights discussed above are few and far between. Often, only one class of good environmental evidence was recoverable, and from a limited time period. This calls into question how representative are the data of the actual state of the environment during prehistoric times. Of course, in this region, one can look elsewhere. Within the Fen and Fen-margin deposits, the complexities of sedimentary succession disguise an enormous potential for abundant environmental evidence on an extensive scale. Above all, there are extensive potentially waterlogged deposits in association with prehistoric monuments.

Sub-alluvial evidence in the lower Welland/Fen margin: Etton, Etton Woodgate, and Borough Fen (Fig. 5.1: Site 2)

Within a kilometre to the east of Maxey and lying just east within the western limit of medieval fen pasture are two unique neolithic sites; an early neolithic ditch bounding a settlement on a microtopographical rise (Etton Woodgate), and within a hundred metres to the east, a middle neolithic causewayed enclosure (Etton). Both sites are sealed by c. 60–130 cm of alluvium, in this case well structured silty clay, which has sealed a more-or-less complete soil profile over an extent of several hectares. Soil micromorphological analysis in progress may be able to establish environmental and land use changes both within and outside both neolithic monuments over a large area or relatively undisturbed prehistoric landscape. Scanning electron microscopy of the alluvium may elucidate the nature, provenance, rate and direction or accumulation of the alluvial deposits.

In acting as a sealing material, the alluvium reduces evapo-transpiration and therefore greatly contributes to the waterlogging of underlying soils and archaeological features. Consequently, organic preservation can be excellent, and can complement the soil evidence. Preliminary pollen analysis of peat from the base of the causewayed enclosure ditch has suggested that the immediate area was open and dominated by aquatic and semi-aquatic plants representative of open water and marshy conditions. Future analyses of macro-botanical remains. insects and pollen from a variety of waterlogged deposits of different dates at Etton and Etton Woodgate, may allow the building of a composite picture of environmental change in the area. Tragically, this evidence has a very limited survival life-time: adjacent dewatering and gravel extraction has lowered the water table on site by up to 1 m. in four months, and the organic remains may be lost within five years (French and Pryor, Society of Antiquaries research project).

The Fen margin areas north and east of Peterborough which are sealed by alluvial deposits are under a continuing threat from drainage operation by the water authorities. Although drainage of this area of the Fens was well advanced by the mid-17th century AD (Darby, 1969), much more severe drainage has occurred since the Second World War as a result of a change in farming policy from mixed but largely pastoral agriculture to intensive arable. For example, until the enlargement of the Maxey Cut in 1953, the Etton area was seasonally flooded and the land suitable only for summer pasture. Now, as the river system is controlled, the area is given over to intensive arable use. In the Borough and Newborough Fen areas further east, pre-alluvial sites located in part of the dyke survey area (see Pryor, this chapter) are often only slightly damp instead of being permanently waterlogged. As we have seen at Maxey, extensive areas of calcareous subsoil comprising river terrace deposits with basic groundwater are not conducive to the continued preservation of organic remains once they cease to be waterlogged. Thus any archaeological sites found in these circumstances around the Fen margin may in effect be "dry" (though nevertheless buried) sites, if not already, then within the decade. Examples within the Fen margin that are now all but "dry" sites are the Borough fen barrows (D.N. Hall's BoF 10 group) and a middle Iron Age fortified enclosure (Scheduled Monument 222). In both cases, only the bases of the ditches remain waterlogged today. Within only a handful of years, the environmental importance of such sites has become progressively limited, and their future is bleak indeed.

Peninsula and island margins in Fenland: Flag Fen (Fig. 5.1: Site 5); Snail Valley

By contrast, pre-fieldwork appraisal of the Fenland topography and sedimentary succession sequences has led to the discovery of many other prehistoric sites in the Fen margin and adjacent Fenland areas northeast of Peterborough which remain waterlogged despite the destructive effects of drainage.

A grid of bore-hole logs taken at c. 0.5 km. intervals as well as a mineralogical assessment report (Booth, 1982) have been made available by the Institute of Geological Sciences. These data give foreknowledge of the underlying topography and sedimentary succession, instead of working blind from the present day flat and ostensibly featureless landscape. One may tentatively construct gross contour maps of the study area at the major stages in fenland stratigraphical history. Combined with the plans of the Anglian Water Authority's dyke cleaning programme which provides ready-cut transects across the landscape, it is possible to empirically predict areas of potentially rich archaeological and associated environmental evidence.

Former margins of Fen sand gravel prominences or "islands" were discerned as areas worthy of closer inspection. Prior to the deposition of the Fen Clay (c. 2700–2200 bc) and subsequently the Upper Peat, many such areas would have been drier and of greater extent, and thus favoured for settlement and other activity. Because the margins of such areas would have been early victims of waterlogging and burial, it is these zones that offer potential archaeological and environmental records of extraordinary quality and scale. Examples discovered to date that confirm this potential include extensive areas of pre-Fen Clay (i.e. neolithic) buried land surface, covering many hectares, which contain earthfast features and artefacts to the north of the Eye gravel peninsula, and a late bronze age wooden platform (Flag Fen: Fig. 5.1: Site 5) in a small peat basin just off Northey Island. A programme of more specific work in association with archaeological evidence, combined with regional pollen studies being undertaken by Dr. A. Alderton for the Fenland Project can only be seen as an as yet unquantifiably important resource for British prehistory.

Other potentially rich areas for combined archaeological and environmental investigation in the Fen/Fen margins, are the sand and gravel banks of former meandering river systems which have since become covered by fen deposits. The Etton and Etton Woodgate sites, for example, sit on opposite sides of just such a stream channel. Further afield, another area of particular interest is the valley of the former River Snail situated in the Fen edge of southern Cambridgeshire (see Crowther and French, this chapter; Hall, 1983).

Conclusions

Perhaps the role of an environmental perspective in field survey design is not always immediately obvious. Certainly the need for an ecological context at the stage of analysis is widely understood, but in the Fenland and Fen margins, the role of the environmentalist and soil scientist is essential from the outset. Given the contextual complexities of the area, it is only with a multi-disciplinary approach in the field that research and rescue time can be spent most profitably, areas of significance isolated, and data capture be maximised.

Many different classes of environmental evidence have been briefly considered from dry, damp and wet locations. Through an integrated study of the whole, many interactive implications emerge. Answers may be provided as to how and why certain classes of environmental evidence are transformed from one state to another. This in turn may help to indicate the possible discrepancies in conclusions that may arise if evidence from dry sites is used in isolation.

A most important *caveat* is that just because a site is in the Fens it will always be wet; only with an understanding of the underlying topography and its changing relationships with the sequence of Fenland succession may the prospection for waterlogged zones or sites be undertaken successfully.

2. Exposure and attrition: an example of dryland archaeological visibility from Maxey, in the lower Welland Valley.
by David Crowther

In general, archaeological survey exploits archaeological visibility. Visibility may mean dislocation, even destruction, of evidence, yet does provide the opportunity to examine pattern on a large scale at minimal expense.

At Maxey (Fig. 5.1: Site 1), where alluvial overburdens were absent, much archaeological evidence was to be found on and in the modern ploughsoil. A variety of survey techniques were applied to 3.75 ha. of this ploughsoil prior to its removal and subsequent excavation of subsoil features. Some of the results have been briefly considered by French, above. Artefact recovery exercises included a metal detector survey across a sample transect (Crowther, 1981) and detailed grid walking across the entire site surface for all finds. A brief summary of the fieldwalking method adopted, its rationale, and some results from the analysis of Romano-British evidence has recently been published (Crowther, 1983). Evidence was presented suggesting that significant intra-site ploughsoil finds patterning is recoverable even on a (flat) site that has witnessed long term, permanent cultivation throughout the historical period. Artefact durability rather than antiquity was suggested to be one of the most important variables affecting the distortion of the record. In the following discussion it will be assumed that the Maxey topsoil flint assemblage, in common with the Romano-British pottery, largely reflects a pattern of deposition, rather than a spatially distorted pattern of post-depositional dislocation.

Figure 5.2 illustrates the subsoil features of this period, together with the gross distribution of ploughsoil surface finds totalling some 107 flints. The subsoil features fall into two stratigraphic phases

a. Cursus monument running along a northwest-southwest alignment
b. Overlying it, a complex of henge with central mound and quarry ditch, together with a mortuary structure/small ovoid barrow at henge entrance

These monuments were, in all probability, "ancient" by the end of the Neolithic. From studies of the soils and stratigraphy, it appears that none of these features were open for very long. The cursus ditches, though massive in extent proved to be of insubstantial construction even allowing for later truncation, with a maximum depth of *c*. 60 cm. Both the central mound ring ditch and the henge circuit ditch had been partially backfilled during the short life of the monument complex. Despite extensive excavation and sieving, there was a notable absence of finds associated with the period of monument building, use, and modification; a few abraded sherds of collared urn were recovered from the final tertiary deposits in the henge circuit ditch. Whatever human activity had been performed within the complex, either it generated no surviving material debris, or much effort was expended on keeping the area clean.

This lack of excavated material is reflected in the topsoil fieldwalking results. Little, if any, of the ploughsoil surface flint assemblage could be confidently assigned to either of the monument-building phases. The nature of this assemblage, comprising squat and side-struck flakes, and piercing/boring type tools, suggests a post-neolithic date; a period for which no subsoil features were found. At Maxey, then, there is an archaeological "phase" of unknown duration, though probably centuries, expressed in the archaeological record as a population of fieldwalked flints. This widely scattered topsoil flint presence, unrelated to any surviving or recognised topographical variation or land division, requires discussion. This phenomenon of widely dispersed lithic "background noise" is by no means unique to Maxey, and its examination could have wider significance for other survey studies of ploughed, flat prehistoric landscapes (*cf*. Holgate, this volume). The potential importance of manuring or "middening", and its significance in terms of land use and rubbish management is now gaining wider acceptance as corroborative evidence grows (Foard, 1978: 363; Wilkinson, 1982; Crowther, 1983). In certain cases the hypothesis is attractive and logical, though in seeking evidence for it in the archaeological record, one must be mindful of certain basic differences in the utility and discard of certain artefact types.

Laying aside arguments about the symbolic role of pottery as a medium whereby status may be conferred upon, or a statement made about, the owner, maker, or its contents, pots in general are essentially made to function as containers. Pottery may protect, hold, support or confine material, either for the purposes of temporary or permanent storage (eg. corn; cremation), or in order to perform activities upon the contents (eg. cooking, consuming). With the exception of certain special forms (eg. the amphora in classical antiquity), the high weight/volume ratio of empty pots and their inherent fragility, imply that they remain comparatively static throughout their useful life apart from certain events in a given pot-life (transportation from point of manufacture to owner/user; subsequent movement associated with change of use/owner).

This rather plodding argument is necessary to emphasise the fundamental difference between the nature and significance of pottery in the archaeological record, and that of flint. In order to justify significant quantities of extra-settlement or off-site pottery fragments, it may be necessary to postulate a deliberate mechanism for its redeposition as secondary refuse. Manuring may be one such possibility. Although the same process of bulk redeposition of domestic or on-site refuse will doubtless embrace many classes of material culture—whether fishing line or flint flakes—the point at issue is whether or not such mechanisms *need* apply to apparently off-site flint distributions. Unlike a pottery vessel, a flint nodule or implement functions in a hand portable, modifiable way and, with the exception of certain exotic types, is apparently disposed of readily. Because the function of a tool or implement is to obtain or modify a resource, it is logical that flint debris, whether a product of flint modification, use, or discard, may occur *in situ* as primary refuse on or off-site. The processes behind flint and pottery entering the archaeological record may be entirely different.

There is striking evidence from a late neolithic settlement area at the Storey's Bar Road subsite at Fengate that flint debris can undergo specialised disposal (Pryor, 1978). A natural hollow in the landsurface had been the apparent depository of sharp—and in a domestic context, undesirable or hazardous—flint working waste that had been dumped or thrown there from a settlement area (Pryor, 1980b). Further evidence which may relate to flint debris discard could be very tentatively implied from some recent work at Hambledon Hill: excavation of soil horizons below and within lynchets of postulated prehistoric foundation were conducted in an attempt to recover artefact accumulations by way of testing a manuring/middening hypothesis. Very few finds of the relevant period were recovered. While the lack of pottery may well be the result of post-depositional attrition, the near absence of flint is noteworthy, suggesting that lithic waste might have been

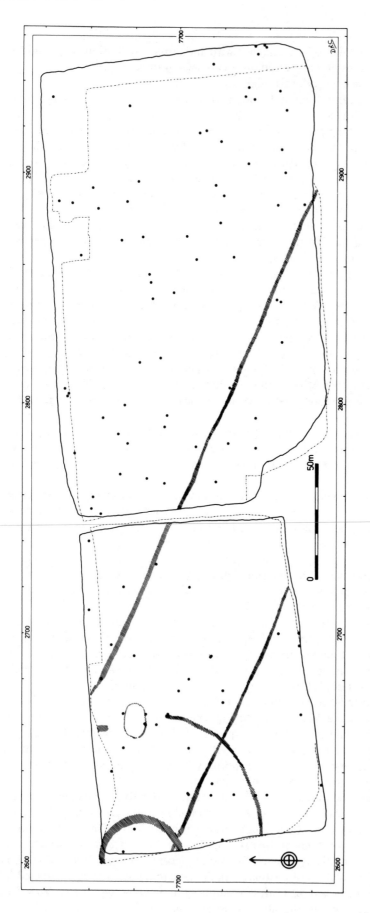

Figure 5.2 Neolithic and bronze age Maxey; subsoil features and ploughsoil surface finds.

66

subject to disposal processes different to other domestic waste, or that working/use/discard may have occurred outside the catchment area of wholesale rubbish management (Mercer, pers. comm.).

Unhappily at Maxey, as with Hambledon Hill, the evanescent nature of early pottery types means their absence in ploughsoil—ancient or modern—may be more illusory than real. The price paid for archaeological visibility in the form of cropmarks and surface finds scatters, and the wider on- and off-site perspectives that result, is of course truncation or destruction of insubstantial structural information, and the loss of whole classes of evidence be they artefactual, environmental, or physiographical. Nevertheless, at Maxey there is good evidence for a change in the status of a study area initially lacking in artefactual evidence during a period of ceremonial monument building and use, followed by a phase of dispersed flint debris discard. While this material may represent a slow accumulation of random flint use and discard off-site across a surface over many generations, it would be clearly dangerous to infer complex patterns of human behaviour across this landscape—or perhaps any other exposed, modern arable landscape—from flints alone. Given the crudeness of the data, interpretation and speculation become barely separable.

This discussion has dealt briefly with two distortions which may affect the material culture as recovered through conventional field survey (or indeed excavation):
a. the possibility of different rubbish management and artefact use strategies between different classes of find; in this case pottery and flint.
b. the extent to which post-depositional processes of weathering and attrition may render heterogenous material culture accumulations (be they structured or unstructured) as mere flint scatters or voids.

The concept of on-site and off-site archaeolgy, and the stress it rightly gives to the continuity of the archaeological record, clearly has wide relevance for understanding human activity and social behaviour across a landscape through time. By definition, the issue can hardly be conceptualised, let alone tested, by site specific excavation, and is one of the most important contributions to archaeological thought that field survey has made. Although this is an issue developing out of field survey and excavation of areas of high archaeological visibility—in this case by widespread arable—the attrition of the data base renders the problem perceived, but insoluble.

One can look elsewhere. The Peat Fens of Cambridgeshire offer a unique combination of archaeological visibility and invisibility, exposure and burial, at various stages of preservation. The potential is therefore there to examine an archaeological record of extraordinary quality over enormous areas. Intact "sites" can be examined as elements within intact landscapes, given the appropriate field survey techniques.

3. Exposure and preservation: a few thoughts on surface and subsurface sampling in the Snail valley—some future work?
by David Crowther and Charles French

The challenge, of course, is in developing those appropriate survey techniques. There are fundamental problems in investigating an archaeological record in a buried landscape. The basic data source is the sample, whether as part of a rigid strategy (of doubtful merit in this context—see Pryor, this chapter) or otherwise. Whatever the exercise, its recovery capacity is going to be very limited. Given the financial and logistical constraints on current (and future) techniques, one may suggest that those questions which stress the continuity of the archaeological record—questions developing out of archaeological visibility, essentially regional in scale—are not appropriate ones to ask of an entirely buried landscape. "Blind" subsurface sampling may record the presence or absence of an archaeological record, though measurement of its nature and extent will be very weak. This need not be a problem, for there other scales of analysis apart from the regional, and these are discussed in section 4 by Francis Pryor. Nevertheless from a pragmatic point of view, at the regional scale, archaeological visibility (in this case peat drainage, desiccation and deflation leading to recent plough damage) may be a sine qua non.

At this point the reader deserves two apologies: firstly, this section offers no discussion of results or performance, for the work has yet to begin; secondly, we will be considering an area outside the lower Welland—Fenland region covered in Figure 5.1.

Some 30 miles to the southeast of Peterborough, on the edge and margins of the southern Cambridgeshire Peat Fenland, the physical geography is undergoing rapid change. Modern drainage and agriculture is causing deflation and desiccation of peats which have sealed an undulating sand and gravel landscape since the Early Bronze Age. The work of David Hall, the Fenland Field Officer in the area, has revealed evidence for intensive early prehistoric activity throughout the third millennium bc and beyond. The density and quality of artefactual material from those areas where the prehistoric landscape is now "popping up" through the peat, is remarkable, and includes burnt clay, burnt and unburnt bone and pottery, as well as lithics. The important recent work that has been done in the area (Hall, 1983) has produced a picture quite different to the one of half a century ago (Fox, 1923, map 1) and, in all probability, a decade ago.

Exposure, and thus archaeological visibility, is therefore a recent phenomenon. Clearly, a multi-disciplinary surface/subsurface examination of a well preserved yet exposed material culture record across a landscape is an attractive proposition, and urgently needed. Relating artefactual, microtopographical, microenvironmental, geochemical and geophysical variation can provide new insights into old data, be it generated in the Welland Valley or elsewhere. However, it is apparent from preliminary work on the ground, that several finds clusters (at any rate in 1982) abruptly disappear beneath the peat as the underlying landscape dips below the later Fen overburden. Here, the archaeology becomes deeply buried, and once more we enter the (literally) sticky ground of trying to monitor variability of unknown complexity via "keyhole" sampling. In this case however, insights into variability are available from abutting exposures. The extensive, though weaker, data set from such exposures, by respecting rather than repressing the spatial continuity of the archaeological record, will help to provide a "handle" for judgement sampling of deeply buried waterlogged contexts which might provide the real "pay dirt" of cultural and environmental evidence of notable quality.

The "damaged" can elucidate the "intact", as well as the other way round. Such may be a compromise solution for cost-effectively investigating at the regional scale, specific areas of Fenland—an archaeological resource of international importance, but sometimes of seemingly intractable obscurity. There are grounds for optimism. With flexibility and experimentation in the field, aids have been, and will continue to be, developed to greatly assist the "visually handicapped" archaeologist. The next, and final, section explores their significance.

4. Fenland dyke survey—its rationale (a question of scale).
by Francis Pryor

David Crowther's discussion of the potential of "dryland", often plough-damaged sites (where surface recovery of artefacts is possible) might be taken as a summary of the current "state of the art". He has stressed the limitations inherent in the various techniques and approaches, and has rightly dwelt upon the daunting taphonomic tangles that must be unravelled—at least in part—if any progress is to be made. One might venture to sum up the problem thus: surface survey can indeed provide a (but not, surely, *the*) picture of ancient activity across a landscape, but we still do not know to what extent it is a reflection of reality. I leave to others to discuss whether our present-day realities are useful or indeed real concepts in the context of archaeology, as she is practised today. It seems to me that the knotty problems surrounding the interpretation of surface scatters of archaeological material can be approached in two ways. First, and perhaps least expensively, one may take a broadly "academic" view; here old data are examined afresh, new comparisons are sought, fresh models are propounded and so on. This is a fine, time-honoured way in which to proceed, but it is not the only approach. An alternative is to seek hitherto unexpected classes of data that just might, given one's field experiences and a liberal allowance of good fortune and intuition, throw new light on the problem. It is an approach that demands flexibility, if for no other reason than one is dealing with the unexpected. One's general aims and intentions must be clear, but the testing of specific narrowly constructed models is impossible within such a research framework (for example Hill's, [1972: 84] "test arguments"). We have also found that certain clearly defined Cultural Resource Management (CRM) objectives—in our case the monitoring of peat surface erosion rates and fluctuating ground water levels—can help to give the research an element of backbone that might otherwise be missing.

David Crowther has already pointed out that the problems inherent in the interpretation of surface survey data may be caused by pre- (cultural) or post-depositional factors. The latter may best be understood (in our region if not elsewhere) from an environmentalist viewpoint: Charles French has already compared the buried landscapes of Fenland with the lighter soils of the Fen-edge and margins. This approach must stress the unity of the whole and it illustrates well the extent to which purely post-depositional factors—such as peat growth, alluviation and marine sedimentation—profoundly affect the way we have to approach our data. Indeed, these effects are so far-reaching that it is often impossible to compare what we assume to be similar types of data—for example flint scatters—in contiguous regions, sometimes within the same square kilometre. Have these relatively simple environmental transformations taken our data beyond mere Schifferian "distortion"? At all events it is often too easy for the archaeologist, concerned mainly with cultural material, to overlook the original unity of the data-base and hence of the information he or she derives from it; we create contrasts and simple oppositions in our search for explanation. In old terminology, "Splitters" rather than "Lumpers", seem to be winning out. For example, at a very basic level, is it true to say that there is always a hard and fast dividing line between pre- and post-deposition? Where does the manipulation of secondary material stop, if at all? These are useful working concepts, but they are no more than that, and unless we are careful they may eventually restrict as much as they presently enlighten.

By this point convention demands that references be made to Theory—surely the most over-used and by now largely meaningless word in the archaeological lexicon. Grasping this nettle, we may outline our

theoretical approach to dyke survey in terms of our immediate practical objectives (so for Theory read Practice throughout). The current state of play may be summarised thus (in no particular order):
1. We seek unexpected classes of data that might answer certain problems encountered in the interpretation of surface survey data, as outlined previously by Crowther;
2. We seek environmental data that might help explain the chronological and spatial patterning of the past communities we are able to identify;
3. We are concerned with problems of deposition and modification, both of the archaeological record (as understood by Schiffer, Foley and others), together with other deposits not immediately obvious as having been affected by man;
4. We must monitor the survival (= destruction) of buried landscapes;
5. We must isolate future areas for study, with an eye both to specific problems and to regions of unexpected potential.

Perhaps these objectives are impossibly lofty and are an excellent illustration of our own naivety, but if they serve no other purpose they do at least illustrate our methodological biases and blind spots. We would like this paper to stimulate comments or torpedoes and will try to respond to either constructively.

The following more detailed discussion of our work is intended to give readers an idea of our project's potential: if we can modify our approach to accommodate another's research interest (without too much trouble), we would be delighted to do so.

It must be apparent by now that our "problem orientation" is diffuse, to vanishing point. We have found, however, that self-imposed blinkers often shut out those types of new data that we seek. By looking at one thing one must ignore another, and archaeologists, like most people, enjoy the familiar. Laying aside practical limitations (cost of travel, depth of water etc.) we *try* to approach our survey with minds as open as we can manage. One might add that this requires as much (or indeed more) discipline as conventional problem-oriented blinkering. It is so easy to follow the obvious—a buried old land surface for example—when one should also be noting the overlying deposits, the modern surface and the buried stream channels in the vicinity; to make matters worse, one must think as one notes. We have come to recognise that hypotheses generated *after* fieldwork cannot be confirmed or modified (would that anything archaeological could be "tested"!) *in vacuo* without conscious or unconscious distortion of the field data. It follows that we should encourage the creation of ideas actually in the field, and that the project should be flexible enough to allow their investigation. Like other simple oppositions, Excavation and Post-Excavation are not invariably useful concepts. The two must be more closely integrated for this (Theoretical?) reason alone; perhaps the spin-off—more prompt publication of results—might encourage the barrier to fall.

So far I have intended to stress what it is that we are *not* doing. Let us continue this negative approach and itemise what it is that our somewhat peculiar region cannot tell us:
1. Fenland consists of enormous spreads of superficial deposits that effectively obscure surface distributions, except around "islands" and the Fen-edge;
2. Only the largest earthworks can protrude through this blanketing material, and even these become totally buried in the deep Fen;
3. Pre-Roman cropmarks are absent on true Fen soils;
4. The region is one of the most intensively farmed in modern Europe;
5. High ground water levels often make dyke survey difficult, dangerous or impossible.

These are some of the reasons why the region has not received consistent attention from prehistorians in the past. It is very difficult to "do" conventional prehistory in such an area: studies of settlement hierarchy, to take a single example, are quite out of the question and the relatively small amount of work that has been carried out (summarised by Godwin, 1978, with references) is decidedly site-specific in its archaeological, if not environmental, scope. It is hardly surprising, therefore, that the only attempt at a regional synthesis has concerned the Roman period where occupation is happily visible, being atop all but the most very recent blanket deposits. Roman earthworks survived until the 1950s (Potter, 1982) and cropmarks are abundantly visible (Phillips, 1970). I do not intend to belittle this major study when I say that it is conventional in its approach; would that one could approach the prehistory of the area in the same way.

Given these practical problems we have decided to begin our study using an old field principle: work from the known to the unknown. In Fenland terms this means that we must move from Fen-edge or island out into the deeper deposits. Our first studies were in the lower Nene/Fen region at Fengate, Peterborough, where there is good archaeological evidence for more-or-less continuous settlement and land use from earlier neolithic times until the massive inundations of the third century AD (for a synthesis see Pryor, 1983a, chapter 8). The site, or sites, however, was surrounded by the urban sprawl of Peterborough New Town which effectively cut Fengate from its hinterland and valley contexts. For comparative purposes we therefore require another, less isolated, area which we could study, with both Fengate and Fenland in mind. A conscious decision was made to study the archaeology and environment of the lower Welland Valley (Pryor, 1980b), as a step towards the deeper deposits further East. That study has been largely finished and the report (Pryor, [ed.] forthcoming) is almost complete. These projects gave us a large and varied data base which we hope can be used as a springboard from which we may enter the Fen. This solid and drift landscape, in geological terms, is known to dip beneath the superficial (Flandrian) Fen deposits gradually. This gentle slope is important as it allows for a slow transition from true "wet" sites (à la Somerset Levels) to "damp" sites in which all surfaces are protected by alluvium and where deeper features contain waterlogged organic material; damp sites become progressively drier as one moves inland, towards the limestone and clay upland of Northamptonshire, Leicestershire and Rutland. Fengate and Etton are good examples of "damp" sites. Inevitably our initial ideas were developed on the dry and damp lands, but these are beginning to change as the result of our more recent research; the causes of these changes may well lie in the unusual nature of the Fen landscape(s) which, we have already seen, may be restrictive in some senses, but enormously liberating in others. Five examples should suffice to show what I mean.

A succession of dated superficial deposits provide a series of tight chronological controls. These deposits are already known in very broad outline but are being re-examined and dated with far greater precision by the D.O.E. Fenland Project's palaeoenvironmentalist, Dr. Ann Alderton. Apart from purely practical archaeological applications—such as the construction of relative chronologies etc.—the successive marine, fluvial and hydrosereal deposits allow us to pinpoint with some precision exactly when moments of archaeological deposition occur or re-occur. Our environmental colleagues' ability to characterise these deposits also provides us with insights as to how or indeed why these events might have taken place.

The frequency and widespread occurrence of these various wet episodes allows accurate stratigraphies to be studied, but over large areas. This allows one to predict where one might find deposits of certain age or indeed, type. One would not expect to find iron age settlement, for example, much below two metres above OD; nor need one seek true "wet" neolithic sites above, say minus two metres OD. Needless to state, the exceptions to working rules of this sort must be of the greatest interest and should actively be sought out.

In certain wetter soils earthworm action is severely restricted and plough-damage is non-existent. These are factors that could allow us to examine archaeological microstratigraphy within buried palaeosols. At least one site (Crowtree Farm; Fig. 5.3) has already been found to exhibit such patterning. The fact that our ancient soils are buried also allows us to determine—using techniques of micromorphology (see French, this chapter)—whether, and to what extent, they have been truncated in antiquity. In certain instances we may also suggest explanations for these events.

Organic material is preserved in wet areas; this now familiar fact allows us to broaden our knowledge of the scope and range of past material culture: fabrics, leather, woodwork and other less expected items (birchbark, string etc.) enormously enrich our picture of the remote past. It is intellectual snobbery of the worst sort to disparage this material simply because it appeals to the imagination directly, without the intervention of graphs or equations. Such material allows us to study aspects of technology usually denied the dryland archaeologist. Finally, wet deposits, usually on "damp" sites, enable us to study *in situ* primary ditch, pit or post-hole infillings before the compaction and distortion that accompanies drying-out has happened. We have found at Etton, for example, that it is a relatively straightforward matter to decide what are the original, middle neolithic, ditch deposits, and at which point secondary, post-neolithic, layers began to accumulate. We are trying to quantify this information which should be of great interest to colleagues working in drier areas.

One final aspect of Fenland that is not always appreciated is that it is base-rich, outside the deeper oligotrophic peat basins such as Holme Fen (Godwin and Vishnu-Mittre, 1975). The principal rivers that drain into the Fen basin carry calcareous run-off and many of the gravels of the western Fen-edge, including those of the Nene and the Welland, contain appreciable quantities of limestone. Thus many of the "damp" sites investigated to date have yielded well preserved bone and molluscs, while at the same time pollen may be found preserved in the waterlogged layers. Such conditions offer enormous opportunities for environmental and economic research.

This brief account of our recent work and the summary of the region's limitations and potential leads us to more immediate concerns. The dyke survey arose from observation of the simple fact that farmers and drainage authorities tend to clean out or enlarge their drainage ditches in the autumn and winter. Almost every field in Fenland is bounded by four dykes and these are usually cleaned out at regular intervals, perhaps every five or seven years. Sometimes this cleaning out is done by hand, in which case the dyke will gradually assume an extended U or Y-shape. Eventually it becomes difficult to maintain such a profile and the ditch is then cleaned mechanically; in these cases the machine operator will slightly deepen the ditch and will cut back the convex sides, to give a clean, open V-shape. This type of cleaning is ideal for our purposes, as it reveals a complete section of perhaps two or three metres' depth. The drainage authorities also carry out periodic drainage improvements which also involve the production of complete profiles; simple ditch bottom maintenance ("slubbing out" or roading) is of little archaeological use.

In an ideal world we would like to examine dykes all over Fenland, but we have neither the time nor the resources to do this. Instead we confine our activities to the Fen and Fen-edge immediately east of the lower valleys of the Nene and Welland (Fig. 5.1). The area chosen for survey is largely arbitrary in extent, the

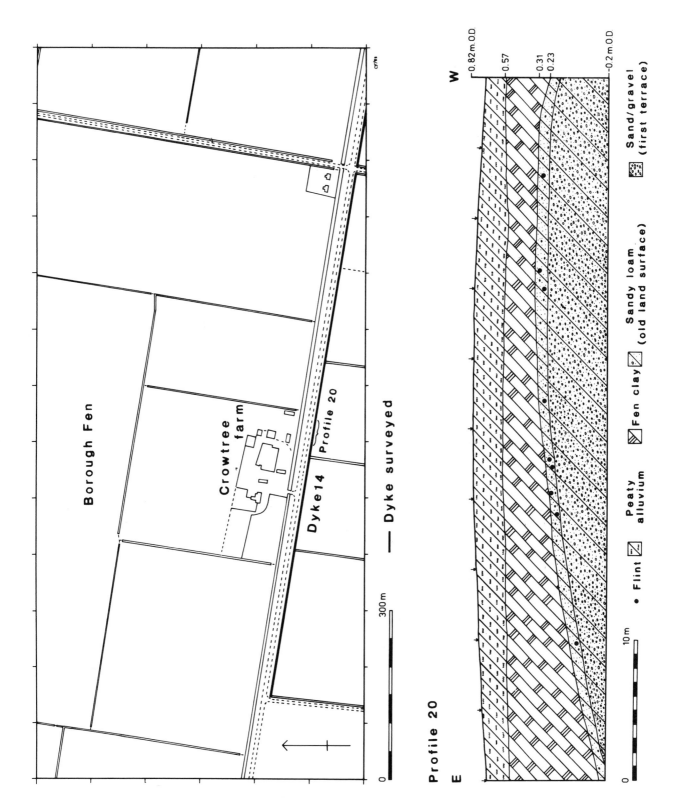

Figure 5.3   Flint micro-stratigraphy at Crowtree Farm.

SW Fen Project   DYKE SURVEY RECORD   Dyke no [   ]

Parish

Grid ref at each end   E [   ] [   ]   E [   ] [   ]
                        N [   ] [   ]   N [   ] [   ]

Landowner

DNH site code(s)
    cut by dyke

    near dyke

Associated surveys   dykes [   ] [   ] [   ] [   ] [   ] [   ]
                      fields [   ] [   ] [   ] [   ] [   ] [   ]

Dyke shape
and parts studied   narrow   wide   other

N
S
E
W

Action   Tick or insert record no where appropriate

Profiles

	1	2	3	4	5	6	7	8	9	10	11	12	13	14	15	16	17	18	19	20	21	22	23	24	25	26	27	28	29	30
Buried landsurface																														
Arch features																														
Finds																														
Extant structures																														
Photoslides																														
Photoprints																														
Drawings																														
Munsells																														
Levels																														
C-14																														
Charcoal																														
Macrobotanical																														
Mag sus																														
pH																														
Phosphate																														
Pollen																														
Snails																														
Soils																														
Wood																														

Notes

Dyke cleaned   198   Dyke surveyed   198   By

Figure 5.4   Dyke survey record sheet.

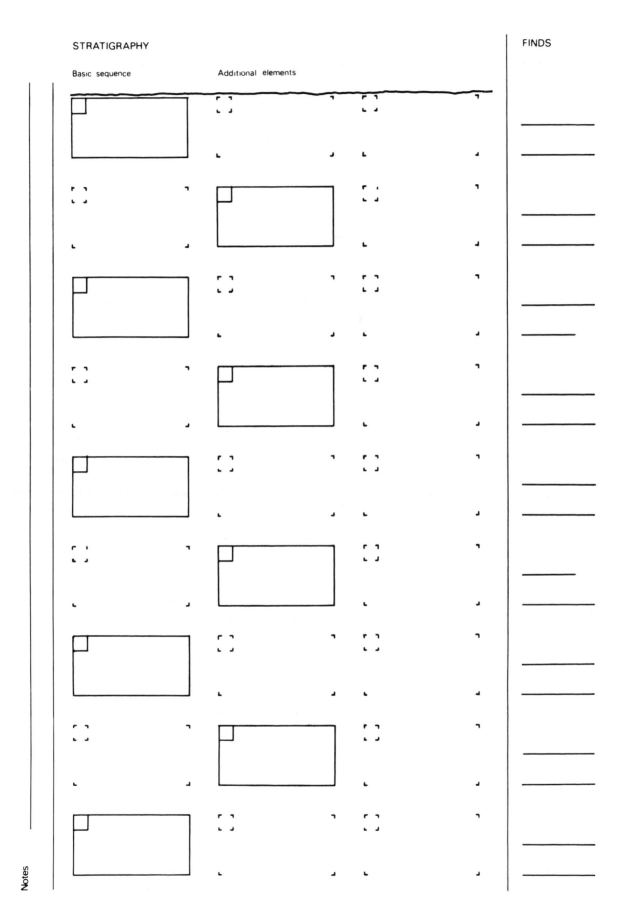

Figure 5.4 Dyke survey record sheet.

principal limiting factors being time, money and distance of travel. In addition to the more intensively studied river gravels of the western Fen-edge, we have also included a complex of "islands" or "peninsulas" around the modern small towns at Eye, Thorney and Whittlesey. Superficial deposits include peats, alluvial peats and organic muds, clay alluvium and brackish or marine silts of mainly neolithic and bronze age date. The underlying, buried, landscape is largely Pleistocene in origin and consists of gravels, sand, clays, or mixtures of all three. In general, the boundary between the two types of deposit is marked by a distinctive band of buried soil.

The basic record is composed of four elements: 25-inch base maps; 35mm colour slides; levelled-in sketches of dykeside sections; notes on the soils and their condition when examined, which are entered onto a proforma dyke record sheet (Fig. 5.4). Every cleaned dyke is examined along its entire length, but only selected profiles are noted in detail. The base map locates every dyke examined and records the position of all profiles. The slides include general views of the dykes and the landscape around them, as well as the profiles themselves; water surfaces are levelled-in and dated.

We have found by experience that it is impossible to make hard-and-fast decisions about the spacing of dykeside profiles. At first we attempted to examine profiles at 50 m. intervals, but soon had to give up when confronted by lengths of dyke stretching for kilometres across featureless expanses of marine silts (where human occupation is, by definition, impossible). In cases such as this we record profiles at intervals of about 150 m. In other cases, for example around the eroding fringes of buried or partially buried islands, we record profiles at every 10 or 20 metres, depending on what is encountered; in areas such as Crowtree Farm (Fig. 5.3) or Flag Fen (Pryor, 1983b) the system of narrow profiles is replaced by a more conventional linear section drawing. However, whatever the sample interval chosen, the full procedure must be carried through: photograph, level, draw, note and map. The levelling is crucial, for reasons outlined above, and each layer interface must be levelled-in as accurately as possible (an easier procedure than measuring down from a fixed point, given the depth of some dykes and the often irregular batter of their sides). The levelling of layer interfaces is intended to be a means whereby we monitor below-ground distortion, if and when we return to the same dykes in future years (clearly a necessity from the point of view of Cultural Resource Management).

Perhaps a word is required at this point on our sampling strategy, or lack of one. The first point to make is that the network of dykes is haphazard, but does conform in its fundamental layout to the region's topography and geology. It cannot therefore be considered as "random" in the strictly probabilistic sense (Stuart, 1976). If it represents a judgement sample, then the judgement exercised was not ours. We therefore see little sense in imposing a pseudo-scientific rigid sampling procedure on a base that is already decidedly flawed; at the same time we try to achieve a reasonably reliable cover of the whole area which is why every dyke, no matter how short, is sampled at least at beginning, middle and end. This also allows us to estimate rise and fall in subsoil layers. The approximate minimum 150 m. sampling interval also helps in these regards.

This somewhat pragmatic approach is also adopted when it comes to the taking of soil samples for phosphate or magnetic susceptibility enhancement analysis; put crudely, if the terrain looks promising, we sample. We originally intended to take geophysical and geochemical samples at regular intervals, but gave up as we simply do not have the time, resources or manpower to do the work. Most samples have to be carried for long distances along wet dykes, together with level, tripod, staff, cameras etc. and we are loathe to do this unless absolutely necessary; besides, experience has shown that these techniques have not yet provided us with substantially new information (thus the magnetic susceptibility equipment does indeed reveal burning, which may also be seen with the naked eye). I suspect that it will require a separately-funded sub-project to evaluate these techniques adequately in the context of dyke survey.

We have found that it is often difficult to predict how long we will take to survey a length of dyke. For example, a two kilometre dyke through one island and extensive alluvial and salt marsh deposits near the village of Newborough took a week to survey, whereas a 400 m. dyke, rich in archaeology (including perhaps three "sites") took three times as long to process. Logistical problems often conspire to slow us down, thus benchmarks vanish, and mapped dykes or field boundaries move (a regular occurrence in Fenland where the only fixed points are the north-easterly winds). But these are problems familiar to all field archaeologists.

A picture is slowly beginning to emerge, but it is not the image we had in mind when we started the campaign in the autumn of 1982. We are not entirely sure what our survey will reveal in the way of "sites" as presently understood; indeed one of our principal short-term objectives is to examine the nature of sites and Foley-style "off-sites"—surely the one implies the existence of the other. If the terms mean anything—and I think they do—then is it possible to provide useful criteria for their definition? Can we define these terms in a region where the preservation of both is equally good? If sites are hard to pin down, settlement patterns and land-use strategies are nearly impossible to grasp. We are given a finely preserved, chronologically precise, archaeologically detailed series of "keyhole" slots into past landscapes. We can say with confidence what will and what will not have survived in less favourable conditions and we can reconstruct the various palaeoenvironments, both micro and macro, with some precision, but in terms of regional survey as presently understood, we are incapable of presenting a comprehensive overall view. We will never do for prehistory of Fenland what has already been achieved for the Roman period (Phillips, 1970). I do not, however, see this as a problem, for there are other scales of analysis at which one may work.

The question of scale may be posed as a summary of the above. Thus the unique qualities of the buried and preserved landscapes allow us to examine micro-level archaeological and taphonomic processes in great detail; it may prove possible to monitor the accumulation of an artefact scatter, or to relate, via long-distance stratigraphy, a trackway to its (also buried) dryland objective. We will be able to see change as a series of separate events, if that was indeed the way things happened; there are also bound to be many more micro-level observations of this sort that the data might suggest to us, providing that is, we are aware of their existence and are able to exploit the opportunities they offer. A "lucky" archaeologist is one who can recognise and then exploit the unexpected; conversely "bad luck" is usually self-inflicted.

We must now pass from the micro-level to the macro-level of analysis, by-passing regional survey except, of course, in the Fen-edge landscapes previously discussed by Crowther. The more general level of analysis is pan-regional, concerned with larger groupings of people and landscapes. Much of this work must be comparative and we maintain close ties with colleagues working in similar regions in Britain and abroad; as with interpretation, we have found it is better to exchange ideas and insights whilst fieldwork is in progress. To broaden one's outlook at the post-excavation stage is merely to gild gingerbread.

In conclusion *(DC, CF, and FP)*

The authors have examined aspects of a data-base, variously preserved, largely as yet ill-understood. This paper has emphasised diversity and flexibility of approach, at the expense of rigidly defined and executed research design. To sum up:

(Rigid) Field Survey Design is fine for those
Who do not wish to follow their nose.
But noses too are sensory tools
That are flexible: so why not break some rules?

Bibliography

Booth, S.J. 1982 The sand and gravel resources of the country around Whittlesey, Cambridgeshire: description of 1:25000 sheets TF20 and TL29. *Mineralogical Assessment Reports Institute of Geological Sciences* 93

Crowther, D.R. 1981 Metal detectors at Maxey. *Current Archaeology* 77: 172–6

Crowther, D.R. 1983 Old landsurfaces and modern ploughsoil: implications of recent work at Maxey, Cambs. *Scottish Archaeological Review* 2(1): 31–44

Darby, H.C. 1969 *The Draining of the Fens*. (2nd edition) Cambridge: Cambridge University Press.

Evans, J.G. 1972 *Land Snails in Archaeology*. London: Seminar Press

Foard, G. 1978 Systematic fieldwalking and the investigation of Saxon settlement in Northamptonshire. *World Archaeology* 9 (3): 357–74

Foley, R. 1981a A model of regional archaeological structure. *Proceedings of the Prehistoric Society* 47: 1–17

Foley, R. 1981b *Off-Site Archaeology and Human Adaptation in Eastern Africa*. Oxford: British Archaeological Reports. International Series 97

Fox, C. 1923 *The Archaeology of the Cambridge Region*. Cambridge: Cambridge University Press

French, C.A.I. 1983 *An Environmental Study of the Soil, Sediment and Molluscan Evidence Associated with Prehistoric Monuments on River Gravel Terraces in North-West Cambridgeshire*. Unpublished Ph.D. Thesis, University of London

Gamble, C. 1982 Review of Foley 1981b. *Proceedings of the Prehistoric Society* 48: 529–30

Godwin, H. 1978 *Fenland: Its Ancient Past and Uncertain Future* Cambridge: Cambridge University Press

Godwin, H. and Vishnu-Mittre 1975 Flandrian deposits of the Fenland margin at Holme Fen and Whittlesey Mere, Hunts. *Philosophical Transactions of the Royal Society London* (B) 270: 561–608

Hall, D.N. 1983 Settlement and ritual areas in the Cambridgeshire Fenlands. Paper presented to Prehistoric Society Spring Conference. *European Wetlands in Prehistory*

Hill, J.N. 1972 The Methodological Debate in contemporary archaeology: a model, In *Models in Archaeology*. D.L. Clarke (ed.) 61–108. London: Methuen

Phillips, C.W. (ed.) 1970 *The Fenland in Roman Times*. London: Royal Geographical Society Report 5.

Potter, T.W. and C.F. 1982 *A Romano-British Village at Grandford, March, Cambridgeshire*. London: British Museum Occasional Paper 35

Pryor, F.M.M. 1974 *Excavation at Fengate, Peterborough, England: The First Report*. Toronto: Royal Ontario Museum Archaeological Monograph 3.

Pryor, F.M.M. 1978 *Excavation at Fengate, Peterborough, England: The Second Report*. Toronto: Royal Ontario Museum Archaeological Monograph 5.

Pryor, F.M.M. 1980a *Excavation at Fengate, Peterborough, England: The Third Report*. Northampton and Toronto: Northamptonshire

Archaeological Society Monograph 1/Royal Ontario Museum Archaeological Monograph 6.

Pryor, F.M.M. 1980b Will it all come out in the Wash? In *Settlement and Society in the British Later Bronze Age.* J. Barrett and R. Bradley (eds.) 483–500. Oxford: British Archaeological Reports British Series 83

Pryor, F.M.M. 1983a *Excavation at Fengate, Peterborough, England: The Fourth Report.* Northampton and Toronto: Northamptonshire Archaeological Society Monograph 2/Royal Ontario Museum Archaeological Monograph 7.

Pryor, F.M.M. 1983b Down the drain. *Current Archaeology* 87: 102–6

Pryor, F.M.M. 1983c Talking heads. *Scottish Archaeological Review* 2(2): 98–100

Pryor, F.M.M. Forthcoming *Archaeology and Environment of the Lower Welland Valley.* Volume to be published by the Fenland Committee

R.C.H.M. 1960 *A Matter of Time.* London: H.M.S.O.

Scaife, R.G. 1983 *An Interim Report on the Pollen from the Etton Causewayed Enclosure Ditch.* Ancient Monuments Laboratory Report No. 3942

Schiffer, M.B. 1976 *Behavioural Archaeology.* London and New York: Academic Press

Simpson, W.G. 1966 Romano-British Settlement on the Welland gravels. In *Rural Settlement in Roman Britain.* C. Thomas (ed.) London: CBA Research Report 7: 15–25

Stuart, A. 1976 *Basic Ideas of Scientific Sampling.* (2nd edition) London: Griffin

Taylor, T.P. 1979 Soil mark studies near Winchester, Hampshire. *Journal of Archaeological Science* 6: 93–100

Wilkinson, T.J. 1982 The definition of ancient manured zones by means of extensive sherd-sampling techniques. *Journal of Field Archaeology* 9: 323–33

6. "One Cannot Dig at Random in a Peat Bog" The Eastern Vale of Pickering and the Archaeology of a Buried Landscape

by R.T. Schadla-Hall and E.W. Cloutman

The Vale of Pickering, especially the eastern end of the basin, to the east of the A64 (Fig. 6.1) has long been recognised as one of the most important areas in Britain for providing information on the late glacial and early postglacial environment (eg. Clark, 1954; 1972; Moore, 1950); the archaeological sites of early mesolithic date within the Vale are of particular importance in European terms. Star Carr (Clark, 1954) has been used as a type site, possibly erroneously (Pitts, 1979), for the Early Mesolithic, and in addition the surrounding area has given indications of containing preserved open late glacial sites (Moore, 1954). The recognition of the importance of the area resulted largely from J.W. Moore's original field work which was based mainly on observations from draining ditches cut through the peat and superficial gravel and till deposits of the Vale, as well as surface observations. Painstaking work by Moore not only resulted in the recognition of Star Carr (Clark, 1949) but also a series of other sites, including the early mesolithic site of Flixton 1, which was excavated by Moore in 1947/48 (Moore, 1950) and the late glacial site of Flixton 2 which was excavated in 1948 and 1951 (Moore, 1954). The complex late glacial and postglacial superficial geology of the Vale, especially in the area under consideration, with kettle holes, eskers and kames as well as moraines and a variety of gravels, clays and calcareous muds has long been recognised to pose several problems of interpretation, and the various postglacial peat deposits which have sealed the area have made interpretation of the early landscape problematical. Moore spent a good deal of time familiarising himself with the late glacial deposits during his original field work, and it is still difficult to produce a coherent picture on the recent geological history of the Vale as a whole (A. Franks pers. comm.).

The nature of the early survey work carried out by Moore is best indicated by his own approach. For example, Flixton 2 was located at the bottom of a "well grassed" ditch face where "some peat is exposed towards the bottom and under the surface of the water. By passing my arms into this basal peat it was possible to examine a large area without recourse to excavation" (Moore, 1950). He isolated a number of sites (Fig. 6.2) by recovering flint from the surface margins of the peat deposits which have been subject to increasing shrinkage and ploughing, especially since the turn of the century, as the various drainage programmes in the Vale have proceeded apace. Moore (1950) pointed out that where such sites were located on exposed surfaces "the incline into deep peat is very rigid and it is likely that the archaeological material scatters out here into the geological deposits". Today the cutting of open drainage ditches and hand digging has ceased; most of the work concentrates on deepening those drains by machine which Moore previously examined, and connecting new subsurface drainage into them, so that opportunities for examining fresh exposures have become considerably less. The original field work carried out in the 1940's and 1950's (Fig. 6.4) emphasised the possibility of recovering a great amount of evidence of late glacial and postglacial activity in the Vale which would be well preserved, relatively undisturbed and indicate, hopefully, a range of sites and responses to local topography and environment. It also underlined the difficulties of recovering such information in a buried wet landscape.

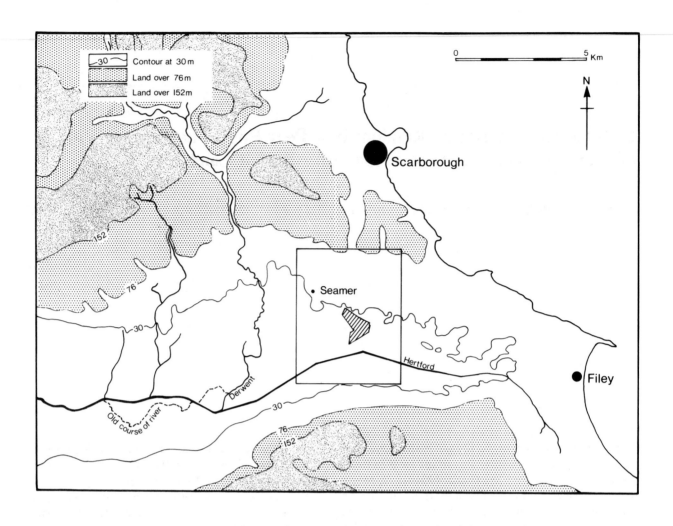

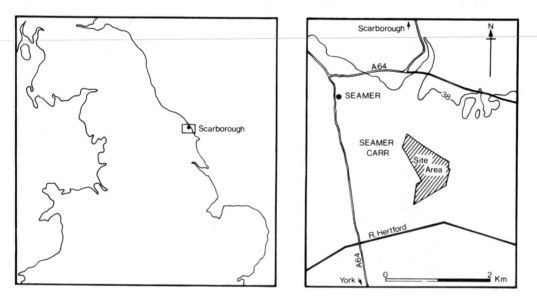

Figure 6.1   The Vale of Pickering and the location of Seamer Carr.

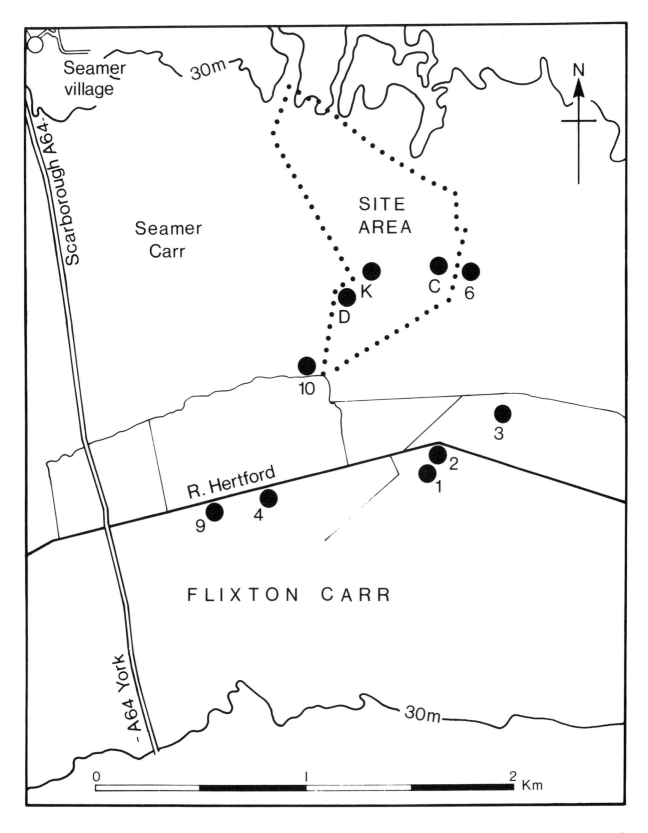

Figure 6.2   The main survey area in the eastern part of the Vale of Pickering. Numbered sites are those located by Moore (1950), lettered sites are those located at Seamer Carr (Schadla-Hall, in press).

The results from the excavations at Star Carr are well known (Clark, 1954; 1972) and as already noted the site was located through the examination of drainage ditches, and selected for excavation as it seemed likely to fulfil a series of carefully formulated objectives (Clark, 1972). At the same time the supporting palaeoenvironmental work in the Vale, which was carried out to fulfil these objectives in conjunction with the excavations at Star Carr (Walker and Godwin, 1954) resulted in a series of borings being taken across the "old lake basin" on the northern margins of the Vale in an area of approximately 6 sq. km. These transects and the resulting stratigraphic and palaeobotanical information not only indicated the likely extent of Zone IV/V peat deposits, but were also used to build up a picture of the early postglacial environment (see Clark, 1954, Fig. 16) and provided a basis for reconstruction of the early postglacial topography. However, with the completion of excavations at Star Carr, in spite of the number of sites recognised in the area by Moore, and the obvious potential richness of the buried landscape, little further work was done in the Vale (Fig. 6.4) and the challenge of continuing the original fieldwork systematically was not taken up.

There seem to have been various reasons for this hiatus. Firstly, the problems of investigating a buried wet landscape were considerable and, in the early 1950's, financial resources were very limited (Clark, 1972). Secondly, the richness of the excavated material at Star Carr and the subsequent worldwide acclaim the excavation received seemed to have reduced further interest in the area, and as Clark (1972) indicated, the original objectives of the excavation had all been met, and no further fieldwork envisaged. Thirdly, by the late 1960's the emphasis in British archaeology was increasingly placed upon the examination of urban areas. Fourthly, the relative lack of resources for archaeology in north eastern Yorkshire (in terms of personnel and finance) meant that comparatively little activity was taking place in the area. Finally, the importance of "off site archaeology" has only recently been emphasised (Foley, 1981) so that the impetus to examine a large, identifiable buried land surface where the process of burial by peat formation was relatively well understood, and the period of post depositional activity could at least be crudely dated, was not particularly great. In addition there was no obvious threat to the buried landscape. From recent, continuing investigation in the Vale it is now possible to show, without doubt, that drainage and ploughing of the peat margins is damaging the preserved archaeological surfaces. For example, at Seamer Carr, (Fig. 6.1) which has escaped major drainage work, the annual fluctuation in the water table exceeds 1 metre, and the marginal areas available for excavation at Seamer are some of the few in the Vale which have not been ploughed. The excavations and palaeobotanical data at Seamer Carr since 1977 have initiated the importance of investigating sites of the same period, but of a different character from Star Carr, and should place the latter in a clearer context (Schadla-Hall, forthcoming).

In 1976 a large area of c. 40 hectares on the northern edge of the Vale was designated a waste disposal plant and dump area by North Yorkshire County Council (Fig. 6.1). In the same year a preliminary survey of the peat stratigraphy was carried out by Dr. E.W. Cloutman and Dr. F.M. Chambers, under the direction of Professor A.G. Smith, in order to identify areas which were likely to contain an early mesolithic site of Star Carr type; Moore (1950) had already indicated that there was evidence for a nearby early mesolithic site (Fig. 6.2). The requirements for such a site were a situation where reed swamp gave way to open water, ideally with these two in close proximity. The results of the detailed stratigraphic survey within the area of the NYCC site showed that reed swamp gave way to open water muds well into the basin in a very deep peat (Fig. 6.3). A pollen diagram showed that the deposits covered the Late Devensian and Early Flandrian periods, and the reed swamp was of early mesolithic date (Zone IV/V). Because of the potential indicated by the initial field survey, and the importance of the site, a committee was formed to advise on various aspects of the work which would need to be undertaken on the site; the bulk of the excavation work, and a large element of the early palaeoenvironmental work was funded by the DoE because of the threat to the site; North Yorkshire County Council also provided help and considerable support.

The immediacy of the threat to the area left little time to develop a strategy for sampling the site, and there was not time to carry out archaeological fieldwork, especially on an area which comprised one of the few under-cultivated areas surviving in the Vale, with no drainage improvements since the 1920's, and where the peat areas were covered in unreclaimed scrubby pasture. As a result, in the first season it was decided to drive a trench into the peat in an area where the palaeoenvironmental information suggested the possibility of recovering evidence for early mesolithic activity. The selected area, Site C (Fig. 6.3), lay on the side of a kame formation closest to the open water deposits mentioned already and on a steeper slope than Flixton 1 or Star Carr. It produced evidence in the form of a flint scatter, and over the next six seasons the area was extended to cover approximately 1,000 sq. metres of buried land surface which yielded over 8,000 worked flints, evidence of hearths and dumps, and a small quantity of well preserved animal bone. This initial discovery, as well as being encouraging also created a number of problems; in terms of crude numbers of flint per square metre the initial sample bore no resemblance to the results from Star Carr or Flixton 1, and there were no comparative excavation results available elsewhere within the Vale. Given the size of the area under threat, and recognising the need to recover "spatial as well as chronological activity" (Foley, 1981)—especially bearing in mind the varied nature of the buried landscape—and the near certainty that the material would be generally related to the eighth millennium BC, it was necessary to develop a strategy to examine the whole of the threatened, buried

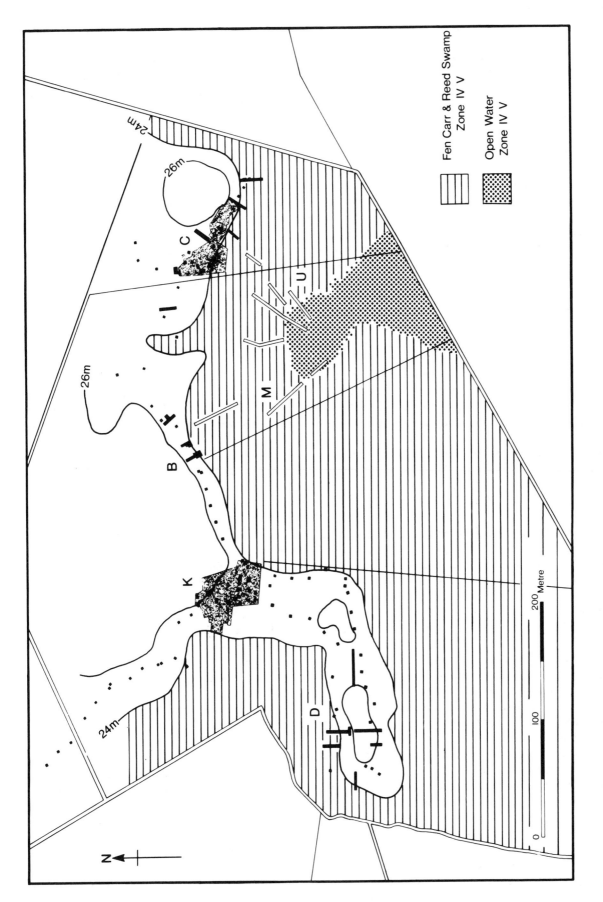

Figure 6.3   The southern part of the Seamer Carr site area indicating the location of sample excavation holes, larger excavated areas and the approximate location of the fen carr and reed swamp, and open water in the Zone IV/V period.

81

landscape in view of the intended total destruction of the area. It was agreed that palaeoenvironmental investigations should continue in parallel with the archaeology and that the date and character of the peats marginal to the basin should be investigated by boring a series of short transects accompanied by several pollen diagrams. The transects were fixed at 15 metre intervals, based on the view that subsurface sampling at this interval would identify any large sites; the rationale behind this interval was based in turn on the size of Star Carr and Flixton 1. The significant observation from the pollen diagrams was that the marginal peats supported a reed swamp/fen carr vegetation during the Early Mesolithic and were not open water. Thus the area excavated at site C produced evidence for activity where a "dry land" flora gave way to fen carr and not where reed swamp bordered open water—a site with completely different environmental characteristics from Star Carr.

The understanding of the main basin margins was further enhanced by means of a detailed contour survey of the muddy sands and gravels which lie directly beneath the peat; the combination of contour survey and stratigraphic sections proved of critical importance for developing the archaeological investigation of the buried surface, and formed the basis for subsequent palaeoenvironmental work. The development of the contour survey resulted in over 100 transects being bored, and the final results have been indispensable for understanding the character of Seamer Carr and its environs.

Based on the distribution of flint scatters recovered from site C, which tended to be found between 24 and 25 metres OD and accepting that it would not be possible to archaeologically survey the whole of the buried landscape, it was decided to carry out sample excavations based on the 15 metre interval transects, placing each test hole to fall on the 25 metre OD subsurface contour, along the entire length of the margins (Fig. 6.3). It was hoped that this would provide comparative information in at least one zone and that the size of each hole (2 x 2 metres sq.) would allow space for a sump for pumping if necessary and also sufficient area in which to work. Over the period 1980/82 just over eighty 2 x 2 m. sq. test holes were cut, and in each case sections were drawn and all archaeological material was recorded. Although it is not appropriate to deal with the results of this work in detail, it is worth noting that over half the test holes produced (not necessarily diagnostic) flint, and that 15 produced either bone fragments or teeth. The sample of the area of buried landscape around the 25 m. OD area of the main basin was under 10% but it did indicate that there is a very high chance of recovering evidence of human activity virtually anywhere within this area. However, only 6 of the test holes produced more than 10 flints per square metre, and flint was used as an indicator of levels of activity. It seemed clear, however, that at least one area required further extensive excavation; site K (Fig. 6.3), which lies away from the main basin was investigated in 1983 because of the large number of worked flints recovered from the test holes dug in 1981/2. On site K after two seasons well over 1,000 square metres of postglacial surface has now been uncovered, with over 8,000 pieces of worked flint and quantities of faunal material; it is also likely that up to another 2,000 square metres of buried land surface exist adjacent to this area which would produce similar concentrations of activity. It is clear that the original sampling approach (see foregoing) based on flint density scatters will not necessarily pick up evidence for smaller "off site" activities. In the case of site C (Schadla-Hall, forthcoming) and also at this stage site K, the sites consist of over-lapping flint scatters with densities as high as 200 pieces per sq. m. Thus the original attempt to survey one zone that centred around 25 m. OD of the buried land surface may well be failing to register a great deal of activity within say the buried land surface between 26 m. OD and 24 m. OD which represents less than 20% of the total area of Seamer Carr. The results of the test holes have however provided some important information, including the implication that flint is far more likely to be found on sandy rather than clayey surfaces within the area, even if a 15 metre interval for test holes may not be ideal for recovering information. It has also become clear as excavation has continued that one of the great values of the Seamer results lies in the possibility of examining large areas of undisturbed, buried post-glacial land surfaces, complete with surviving faunal and flint assemblages.

The 2 x 2 metre test holes are unfortunately not applicable over the whole area. Much of the buried land surface at Seamer Carr, and elsewhere in the Vale, lies under more than 2 metres of peat and it is unlikely that it will be possible without extremely expensive pumping apparatus to examine these areas using those test holes. One particular part of the Seamer Carr site in the south east of the area which was identified as containing an open water/reed swamp edge zone, was identified for waste dumping in 1983. It was obviously an area well worth examining, and the buried surface lay under up to 3 metres of peat. The solution to the problem, at short notice, was to use a tracked excavator to cut a series of sections across the reed swamp/open water zone, which was located by boring. The upper peat deposits were dumped on one side of the machine cut trench, and the lower deposits containing the calcareous muds on the other; the material from the lower peats was then examined by hand, and in one area twelve fragments of bone were recovered from one of the 1 metre wide sections, which at least tended to suggest a larger deposit in that area. It has proved impossible to follow up this particular discovery, and much of the area is now being dumped over, but it does serve to underline the problems of excavating the deep peat in economic terms, or at least at a reasonable cost. It also indicates the potential for other areas of the buried land surface.

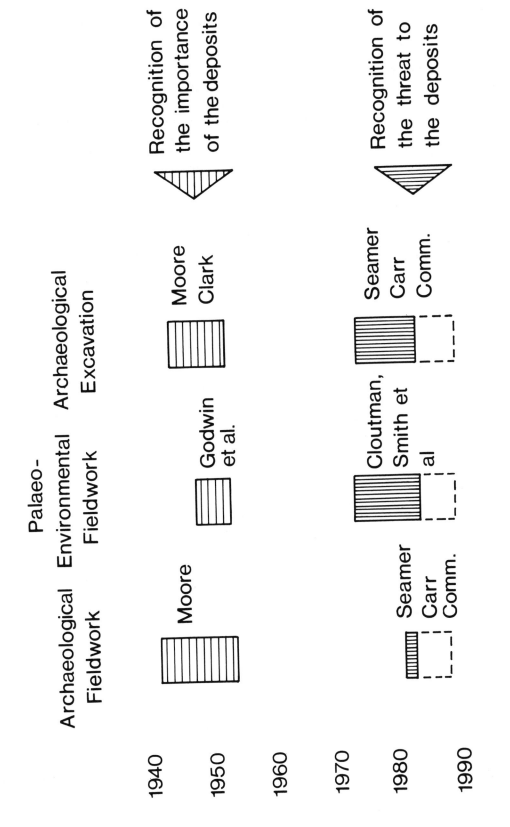

Figure 6.4   The development of field survey and excavation on the buried landscape of the eastern Vale of Pickering 1930–90.

The problem at Seamer Carr will remain the difficulty of evaluating the results of the archaeology. This is even with the availability of the data from stratigraphic and subsurface contour work relating to the buried landscape, given the limited sample of archaeological survey work which tends to relate to one specific zone within a 40 ha. area. Nevertheless, the initial period of work which has mixed survey with excavation (Table 6.1) has provided data about large areas of buried early mesolithic land surfaces. The scale of excavation is probably greater than elsewhere in Europe and has not only indicated the scale of this landscape, but also the problems which sample surveys can create. Certainly neither boring nor 2 metres square test holes alone have produced a clear picture. The results from the excavations can be used however to provide a body of information for further survey work and hopefully the production of more coherent survey designs (Table 6.2). The main result of the survey work at Seamer has been to emphasise the importance of palaeoenvironmental investigations based on detailed stratigraphic surveys of the peat deposits accompanied by at least skeleton pollen diagrams and radiocarbon dating. The transects combined with the recovery of the buried landscape, when examined against the information being accumulated on site location, should allow some level of prediction about the location of other sites. At Seamer it has been possible to identify activity locations adjacent to reed swamp, on dry land, on isolated islands, and possibly on the edge on open water, as well as in the case of site K, in areas apparently cut off from the main basin.

Table 6.1:   The development of field survey work at Seamer Carr 1976–84

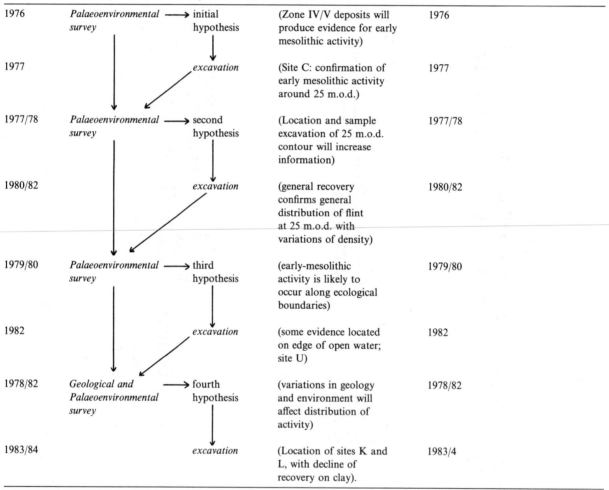

1976	*Palaeoenvironmental survey* ⟶ initial hypothesis	(Zone IV/V deposits will produce evidence for early mesolithic activity)	1976
1977	excavation	(Site C: confirmation of early mesolithic activity around 25 m.o.d.)	1977
1977/78	*Palaeoenvironmental survey* ⟶ second hypothesis	(Location and sample excavation of 25 m.o.d. contour will increase information)	1977/78
1980/82	excavation	(general recovery confirms general distribution of flint at 25 m.o.d. with variations of density)	1980/82
1979/80	*Palaeoenvironmental survey* ⟶ third hypothesis	(early-mesolithic activity is likely to occur along ecological boundaries)	1979/80
1982	excavation	(some evidence located on edge of open water; site U)	1982
1978/82	*Geological and Palaeoenvironmental survey* ⟶ fourth hypothesis	(variations in geology and environment will affect distribution of activity)	1978/82
1983/84	excavation	(Location of sites K and L, with decline of recovery on clay).	1983/4

To some extent at least, the survey work at Seamer Carr has involved relearning from work which went on over 30 years ago and then to build on this. A further programme by Professor A.G. Smith and Dr. E.W. Cloutman has now been developed for an area of approximately 6 sq. kms. of the Vale using techniques similar to those used at Seamer Carr to examine the buried topography and peat stratigraphy. This work should make it possible to reconstruct the Zone IV/V palaeoenvironment indicating areas of dry land, open water, reed swamp and carr. Attention will be concentrated on the basin margins but sections will be made through areas deeper in the basin when necessary. Once the initial process of survey is complete, test holes will again be placed in those areas where it seems likely that evidence for early mesolithic activity can best be recovered, as well as in some areas as a control, where it is assumed there will be no archaeological evidence at all. Whilst this palaeoenvironmental work, funded by the SERC, is in progress, it is also intended over the next two to three years to carry out a field walking programme along the peat margin in an attempt to locate further evidence of early mesolithic activity in ploughed areas (Table 6.2).

Table 6.2: The development of a survey strategy for investigating the buried landscape in the eastern Vale of Pickering.

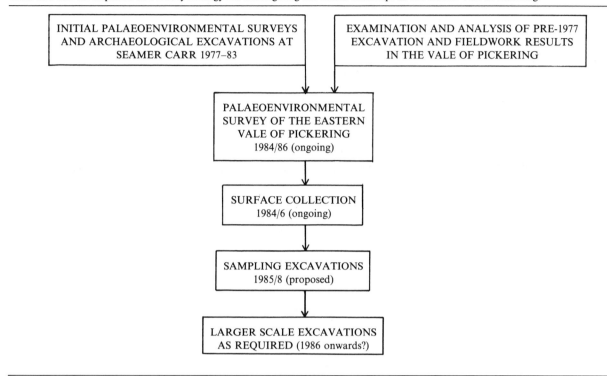

There is still a considerable amount of work to be done in investigating the buried postglacial and possible late glacial landscape of the Vale (J.W. Moore pers. comm.). None of the techniques used and outlined here are new, only their combination and their application, sustained over a long period and on such a scale. Nor has information usually been sought in such detail; for example the approach to contouring the buried landscape and combining it with detailed environmental reconstruction has never been attempted previously. Test excavation in several areas of the Vale may still prove difficult, and the fluctuating water table will always be a problem for excavation even if the Vale is drying out. It still remains difficult to suggest a target population of sites or rather "off sites" (Foley, 1981) because there are no comparative attempts available for a survey on such a scale dealing with a buried landscape that are known to the authors, and there is no doubt that the questions we seek to answer are those which Cherry and Shennan (1978) dealt with (i.e. how many sites, what distribution and function within the various environments do they have, and what relationships are there between the sites?). If the approach we have outlined succeeds then the information recovered should allow the results to be extended to other areas and ought to produce enough data to advance our understanding of the Early Mesolithic in an area where the advantages of a buried landscape far outweigh the problems of examining it.

Acknowledgements

For help, advice and discussion, A.G. Smith (who is also overall supervisor for EWC's work), P.A. Mellars, A.G. Franks, J.W. Moore, R.K. Simpson and T.C. Ray. For initial palaeoenvironmental survey work, F.M. Chambers, and to N. Munson, L. Moffet, J.S. Cloutman and G.T. Wimble who acted as field assistants in the palaeoenvironmental surveys. To M.J. Millett, for his help, and to M. Griffiths and D.W.A. Startin for support. The drawings are by R.K. Simpson.
    Note: The title of this paper– "One cannot dig at random in a peat bog" was taken from a letter by J.W. Moore to the New Scientist (21st July 1983).

Bibliography

Cherry, J.F. and Shennan, S.J. 1978 Sampling cultural systems: some perspectives on the application of probabilistic regional survey in Britain. In *Sampling in Contemporary British Archaeology*, J.F. Cherry, C. Gamble, and S.J. Shennan (eds.) pp. 17–49. Oxford: British Archaeological Reports British Series 50

Clark, J.G.D. 1949 A Preliminary Report on Excavations at Star Carr, Seamer, Scarborough, Yorkshire, 1949. *Proceedings of the Prehistoric Society* 15: 52–69

Clark, J.G.D. 1954 *Excavations at Star Carr*, Cambridge: Cambridge University Press

Clark, J.G.D. 1972 *Star Carr: A Case Study in Bioarchaeology*, Menlo Park, California: Addison-Wesley Publications 19

Foley, R. 1981 Off-site archaeology: an alternative approach for the short-sited. In *Pattern of the Past*, I. Hodder, G. Isaac and N. Hammond (eds.) pp. 157–82. Cambridge: Cambridge University Press

Moore, J.W. 1950 Mesolithic sites in the neighbourhood of Flixton, North-East Yorkshire. *Proceedings of the Prehistoric Society* 16: 101–8

Moore, J.W. 1954 Excavations at Flixton, Site 2. In *Excavations at Star Carr*, J.G.D. Clark pp. 192–4. Cambridge: Cambridge University Press

Pitts, M.A. 1979 Hides and antlers: a new look at the gatherer-hunter site at Star Carr, North Yorkshire, England. *World Archaeology* 11: 32–42

Schadla-Hall, R.T. forthcoming The early postglacial in Eastern Yorkshire. In *Archaeology in Eastern Yorkshire*, T.G. Manby. (ed.)

Walker, D. and Godwin, H. 1954 Lake Stratigraphy, pollen analysis and vegetation history. In *Excavations at Star Carr*, J.G.D. Clark pp. 125–69. Cambridge: Cambridge University Press

7. Survey of a Settlement: A Strategy for the Etruscan site at Doganella in the Albegna Valley

by Lucy Walker

Introduction

This paper examines the problems in surveying an individual site by reference to the site at Doganella in South Tuscany, Italy.

During an Interval survey of the Albegna Valley (Fig. 7.1), an area enclosed on three sides by a sub-rectangular crop mark spanning some 240 hectares (590 acres), was found to be densely scattered with artefacts. The site would seem to correspond to what the nineteenth century Etruscologist, George Dennis, found and described as a walled Etruscan city. He recorded that in the 1840's no ruins were visible above ground, but that the site was recognisable by the amount of pottery lying in the fields (Dennis, 1878: 263–266).

Mauro Michelucci has recently conducted two small excavations at the east end of the site, and suggests that the settlement developed in the late sixth century and was suddenly and violently destroyed in the mid fourth century BC. He recorded two successive building phases within that period (Michelucci, 1981: 102; Excavation report in press).

The site lies on a gently undulating terrace north of the wide Albegna flood plain. Its lowland setting in the predominantly arable fields around the sparsely settled village of Doganella, renders it almost entirely accessible to field survey, whilst at the same time, current deep ploughing is ensuring its complete destruction.

Given these conditions therefore, and the apparent size of the site, it was felt appropriate to make use of the enormous data resource in the plough soil, and to survey the rest of the area, recording the spatial distribution and association of artefacts over the whole site. It was our intention to use survey techniques to determine the size and layout of the settlement, and to explore details of its internal organisation within a spatial-behavioural framework (Clarke, 1977: 1–32; Schiffer, 1976).

Field survey is usually considered most appropriate for regional analysis of settlement and land use patterns. It is less commonly used for 'within site' work, where detailed spatial patterning is generally explored by excavation, even though the latter may only be possible in a limited area of any settlement.

This paper raises some of the problems encountered when a methodological approach tailored to suit a broader level of resolution is used to examine spatial patterning in a more detailed context. It suggests how these problems may be resolved, and illustrates how they are being tackled at the site at Doganella.

Discussion

Problem areas

The survey team encountered three main problem areas which are inter-related, and can be expressed in terms of the following questions:

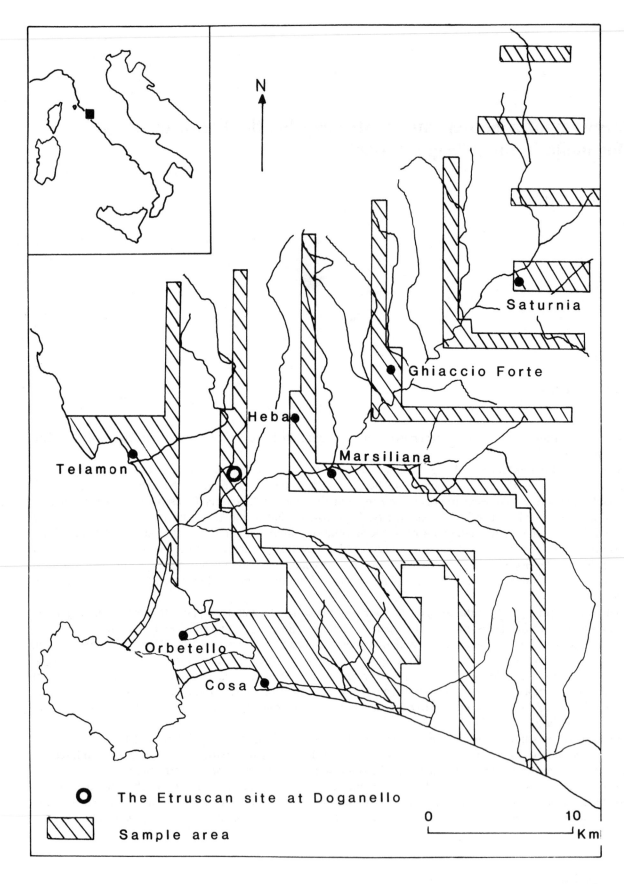

N

Saturnia

Ghiaccio Forte

Heba

Marsiliana

Telamon

Orbetello

Cosa

○ The Etruscan site at Doganello

▨ Sample area

0   10
                    Km

Figure 7.1   The Albegna Valley-*Ager Cosanus* Survey area, in south west Tuscany, with an inset location map of Italy.

1. What is the relationship between data collected from surveying the topsoil, and the data which might have been collected through excavating features in the subsoil?
2. At what level of resolution, or with what degree of precision should we observe and record the archaeological data?
3. What should be our sampling strategy within the sample framework adopted? This applies both to the area of ground to be surveyed and to the artefacts to be retrieved.

Both questions two and three can only be resolved by a decision about what type of information is required, or is possible to obtain, from the data. Without an awareness of the site formation processes however, which relates to question one, it is not possible to be clear about what degree of recording precision would be appropriate over the site, or even what spatial patterning is wished to be perceived.

The first question highlights how the data set cannot be treated in the same way as an excavation plan because the formation processes of the archaeological record are different. A ploughed site, for example, whilst apparently "offering" a visible artefact population to record on the soil surface, presents the problem of how to sample and interpret the topsoil components in relation to the underlying deposits, both being "unknown" populations subject to variable amounts of damage and displacement. This "unknown" factor will be exacerbated by differential land use over the site.

Moving towards a solution

We need predictive models about what the archaeological record on the soil surface might actually represent, in order to formulate a recording and retrieval strategy, and to enable us to interpret the surface scatters. These models must apply both to the cultural formation processes, and to the post depositional processes to which the former have been subjected.

Taking the cultural formation processes of any settlement, the potential 'on-site' units of analysis may be simplified into two components:

i. The individual buildings, features or 'activity' areas which go to make up:
ii. The site, or community itself.

Within this framework, it is possible to identify areas of interest by considering the factors which could be studied within the various spatial matrices of these two broad levels of resolution (Clarke, 1977: 1–32; Trigger, 1968: 53–78). It is then however necessary to clarify what sort of information may be retrieved by considering how these factors influence the archaeological record (Schiffer, 1976), and which elements may be represented in the plough soil.

On ploughed sites, the archaeological record may be divided into two main components: the topsoil and the subsoil contents. In principle, therefore, it is possible to predict the difference between the excavated data set and the survey data set: as the topsoil is generally removed by a bulldozer prior to excavation, the former will be be made up of one component, that is, the truncated subsoil components. The latter will be made up of both topsoil and some subsoil components, and their relative composition will depend on topography and land use.

In general, subsoil features will include building foundations, burials and *secondary refuse* of all periods. The data set on the surface of the ploughsoil however, will also be expected to include *primary refuse* of all periods and a large quantity of *de facto refuse* (abandoned artefacts) from the final period (Schiffer, 1976: 30–34). The latter will comprise artefacts left *in situ* in their places of production or use, and abandoned building debris.

At Doganella, for example, survey has established that the archaeological record in the ploughsoil is dominated by a blanket of culturally similar settlement debris, including copious amounts of stone building rubble, roof tiles, and ceramic vessels within the building debris. It is suggested that this is predominantly *de facto refuse* from the period when the site was abandoned (Michelucci, 1981: 102). It is possible to distinguish these clusters of *de facto refuse* from the more sparse, abraded background noise of discarded debris, and from the *secondary refuse* features such as pits. The latter may be identified by patches of distinct dark organic soil containing a relatively higher diversity and density of materials, particularly pot sherds and bones, within a more confined area. It is, in fact, precisely these distinctions which validate a detailed 'on site' survey of spatial relationships.

Turning to differential factors of landuse and topography: on a ploughed site, the amount of subsoil features represented in the topsoil will be affected by the extent of the accumulation or loss of soil over the site, and the depth and strength of the plough action. The extent of horizontal displacement is dependent on inter-related factors such as the direction of the plough action, the variety of slope, and weather conditions. All these factors will affect the stability and downslope erosion of soils, and the differential movement and survival of artefacts. It is therefore vitally important to combine a survey of the surface scatters with a land use and geomorphological survey.

Survey Strategy at Doganella

Owing to the enormous size of the site, and the lack of an adequate data base upon which to formulate a detailed research strategy, it was decided to:

i. Extend the 1 km. wide north-south Interval Transect of the regional survey to include the whole site and to increase the area of hinterland under study (Fig. 1). This strategy has been adopted for all known population centres within the broader regional survey (Fentress and Celuzza, 1980: 1).

ii. Adopt a two tiered 'on site' survey approach, to enable the team to work from a coarser to a finer scale of resolution where appropriate.

Stage 1, with relatively rapid, but systematic survey techniques was planned as an initial *extensive* survey over the whole area available. Stage 2, in response to the results of stage 1, could involve a more intensive survey of sample areas. It would then be possible to focus on particular research questions highlighted by the initial extensive survey, and step up the level of resolution in selected areas where it is considered that information could be retrieved from a more precise observation of spatial relationships. The more detailed exploration of particular spatial associations within zones of the settlement, or functions within buildings, would require finer gridding and retrieval strategies than is appropriate for stage 1.

Stage 1 Strategy

A survey of the geomorphology and land use of the terrace has been combined with a survey of the distribution of the surface scatters of archaeological material, in order to:

i. Acquire a comprehensive overview of the site formation processes, and to assess the relative components of the archaeological record over the site as a whole.

ii. Explore the broad spatial patterning within the perceived clusters of archaeological material, establishing the size and general layout of the settlement, defining areas of activity, and clarifying its chronology.

It has taken a team of five people approximately four weeks to systematically fieldwalk about two thirds of the terrace and its slopes (Fig. 7.2): an area of about 250 hectares (612 acres). Although we await a detailed analysis of the retrieved artefacts, a discussion of some of the spatial patterns perceived in this first stage extensive survey may be found in Walker (1985). The results will be published more fully in the Albegna Valley-*Ager Cosanus* Survey Report.

We are fortunate that the geomorphology of the area has recently been studied by a team from the Department of Physical Geography and Soil Science, Amsterdam, who have carried out a detailed soil survey of the region (van Berghem *et al.*, 1984). In addition, in association with the archaeological survey at Doganella, soil scientists from the same department have analysed soil formation processes and the extent of erosion and displacement over the site. They have also augered soil profiles in specific features, notably the cropmarks and contours around the settlement (Fig. 7.3). Where possible undisturbed soil profiles revealed by modern cuts (roads, drain pipes etc.) were examined: when these were associated with subsoil features it was possible to ask questions about the contemporary environment and land use.

For field walking and recording purposes, the land use survey has enabled us to divide the area into three main categories: these are illustrated in Figure 7.2.

i. Deep ploughed fields normally under cereal cultivation, offering maximum visibility and a complex data set, with both subsoil components as well as *de facto refuse* represented in the topsoil.

ii. Areas under crops or low vegetation such as vines, tomatoes, vetch, stubble and pasture, where, although the land is accessible, visibility is impaired. In addition where the ground has not been subjected to the regular 'deep plough' treatment the surface components are qualitatively and quantitatively distinct from category (i).

iii. Areas so far inaccessible due to the presence of buildings, yards, roads, cereal crops (unharvested in the survey period), and unhelpful land owners.

Stage 1 Fieldwalking

1. Level of resolution of observation, recording and artefact retrieval.

In accordance with the objectives of the first tier programme, the entire area available in land use categories (i) and (ii), has been systematically field-walked in strips, by a team of people spaced at 4–5 m. intervals. No area was grid surveyed but surface clusters are measured by pacing and estimates. They are sketched, and carefully

Figure 7.2 Doganella: the area covered in the first stage extensive survey. The interval survey transect has been extended 1 km. to the west. The land is divided into three main land-use categories, which affect the data set available to the surveyor:

(i) Fields marked as ploughed are all deep ploughed for cereal cultivation, affording maximum visibility and accessibility, whilst at the same time being subjected to maximum plough damage.

(ii) Ground covered with low vegetation, including stubble, vetch and tomatoes, and vines, subjected to variable plough damage and although accessible, offering impaired visibility and an inconsistent data set.

(iii) Inaccessible areas, not surveyed due to the presence of buildings, roads, or dense harvested crops.

located on the map with the aid of a prismatic compass, topographic features, and the regular rows of olive trees which are also recorded on air photographs.

Each perceivable cluster or 'sub-site', is given a site or identity number, and its general characteristics described on a record sheet. These include details of topography and soils, as well as the broad composition of the archaeological material, and the distribution of artefacts. A judgemental sample of 'representative' artefacts is retrieved from each sub-site.

Owing to poor visibility over much of the area in category (ii), it was not feasible to do much more than determine the presence or absence of artefacts on the ground. Retrieval was also a much more 'hit and miss' affair. In the deep ploughed fields of category (i), however, although there has been substantial soil and artefact displacement on the slopes, spatial clustering is still quite distinct. The dispersal of artefacts is to some extent mitigated by the consistent forward and return direction of the plough, determined by the lay out of the olive trees. It is in these fields therefore, that the archaeological record would be most susceptible to a more detailed observation of spatial patterning.

2. Artefact sampling.

There were three dominant criteria for our retrieval strategy: firstly, the data set is so extensive that total surface retrieval was absolutely out of the question. It would pose severe handling and storage problems if such a policy were carried out even on one 'sub-site'.

Given this overwhelming practical consideration, it was felt that it would be most appropriate for the first tier extensive survey, to retrieve a sample of artefacts diagnostic of (i) activity, and (ii) chronology. Within these parameters the pottery was where possible sampled for rim, base and handle sherds.

It should be stressed that the retrieved sample is not an indicator of the relative quantities of these components of the data set in each sub-site. Such information could only be retrieved by a controlled grid survey and sampling strategy, and would be more appropriate for a research strategy in stage 2.

Selection according to activity did not present a particular problem. We worked on the principle that the retrieved sample should reflect the maximum number of activities which were perceived in the surface debris. This included building, living, eating, discarding, food-processing, storage, smelting, weaving and pot manufacturing. Where these were represented by ceramic artefacts with macroscopically distinct fabrics, samples of the different fabrics were also retrieved. At a higher level of inference, these artefacts may be related to levels of technology, trading, relative status and wealth.

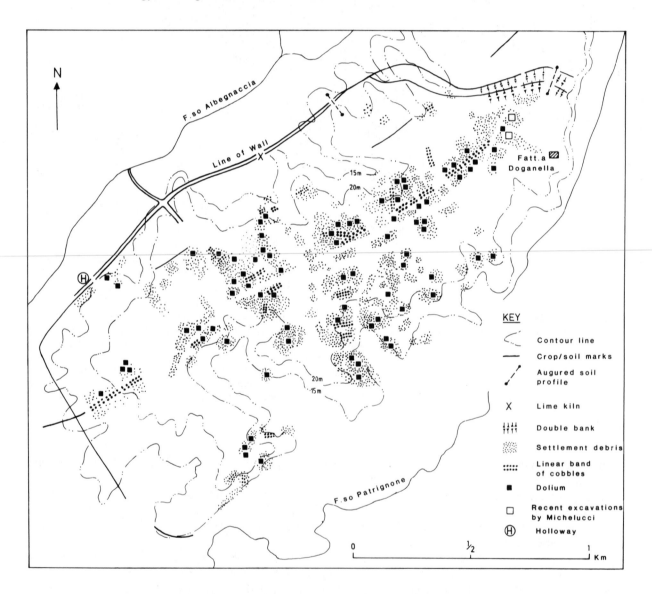

Figure 7.3   Spatial patterning observed: the topography of the site, and the surface distribution of artefacts, including stone building rubble, cobbles, tiles and pottery. The *dolia* (large storage jars) have been singled out to illustrate their ubiquity over the site. (For a discussion of the spatial patterning see Walker, 1985). Two places are indicated where soil profiles have been analysed across the crop marks surrounding the site.

Figure 7.3 indicates the distribution of settlement debris perceived over the site so far surveyed. This is characterised by unfaced stone, cobbles, ceramic roof tiles and pottery. Figure 7.4 illustrates the distribution of artefacts associated with particular crafts and industries.

Selection according to chronology however, proved to be more of a problem for two main reasons. Firstly, the difficulty of dating some ceramics, particularly coarsewares. Secondly, both the archaeological record and our recording strategy was biased towards the clustering of *de facto debris*, presumably from the final building and occupation phase of the site. This is likely to be both more abundant and generally less abraded than the debris of earlier periods. The construction of a chronological framework is further exacerbated by the difficulty in ascertaining exactly how much of the underlying stratigraphy has been caught by the plough share, and therefore what is likely to be represented in, or missing from, the top soil. These points emphasise the important interdependence between survey and excavation. We need long and reliable stratigraphic sequences to enable surveyors to recognise diagnostic artefacts, and we also often need a stratigraphic "window" to clarify a sequence which may not be detectable on the surface.

At Doganella, it would probably be most appropriate to maximise a random sample over the site, and compare this data with the stratigraphic information which Michelucci is now producing.

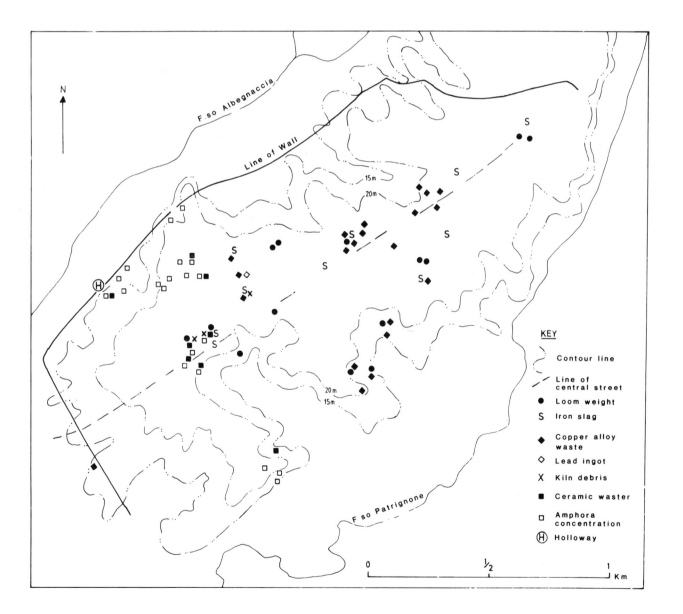

Figure 7.4 Spatial patterning: the observed distribution of artefacts associated with weaving, metal working, and the production and storage of *amphorae*. I have argued (Walker, 1985) that their contrasting distribution is economically significant.

Conclusion

This paper has raised three of the main problems which characterise the bridging position occupied by 'on site' survey between regional survey and excavation, an area where methodological models are still being developed. The attempt to resolve these issues at the Etruscan site at Doganella has highlighted two main points:

i. The need for an awareness of the site formation processes. This is not only of fundamental importance in the process of interpreting the observed data, but is also integral to the choice of survey strategy.

ii. The need for stratigraphic sequences derived from excavation, to enable inferences to be made within a chronological framework. While survey can provide an important record of spatial patterning over a large area, our interpretation of the data is also dependent on the stratigraphic information and control afforded by excavation.

Acknowledgements

I would like to thank everyone who has been, and still is, involved with the survey of the site; and also Martin Jones and the editors of this volume for reading and commenting upon an earlier draft of this paper.

The Albegna Valley-*Ager Cosanus* Survey was initiated by Professor Andrea Carandini (Pisa University), and is co-ordinated by Maria Grazia Celuzza (Grosseto Museum) and Elizabeth Fentress (Siena University). It is supported by the Sette Finestre Committee with British and Italian funding. The 'on site' pedological analyses have been carried out by Jan Willem van Berghem, and Pieter Windmeijer (Amsterdam University).

Bibliography

van Berghem, J.W., Meijvogel, T. and Windmeijer, P. 1984 *Soil Survey of the Albegna Valley in S.W. Tuscany, Italy*. Vols. I and II, and Appendix I (Soil Map). Fysisch Geografisch en Bodemkundig Lab.: University of Amsterdam

Clarke, D.L. 1977 Spatial Information in Archaeology. In *Spatial Archaeology*. Clarke, D.L. (ed.) pp. 1–32 London: Academic Press

Dennis, G. 1878 *Cities and Cemeteries of Etruria II*. London: Dent

Fentress, E. and Celuzza, M.G. 1980 *Survey in the Ager Cosanus and the Albegna Valley: Interim Report, 1980*. London: Institute of Archaeology

Michelucci, M. 1981 Magliano. In *Gli Etruschi in Maremma*, M. Christofani (ed.) pp. 101–106. Milan: Sivona

Schiffer, M.B. 1976 *Behavioral Archaeology*. New York: Academic Press

Trigger, B.C. 1968 The Determinants of Settlement Patterns. In *Settlement Archaeology*. K.C. Chang (ed.) pp. 53–78. Palo Alto: California National Press

Walker, L.M. 1985 The site at Doganella in the Albegna Valley: Spatial Patterns in an Etruscan Landscape. In *Papers in Italian Archaeology IV Part iii Patterns in Protohistory*. S. Stoddart and C. Malone (eds.) British Archaeological Reports International Series 245: 243–254

8. Settlement, Economy or Behaviour? Micro-regional Land Use Models and the Interpretation of Surface Artefact Patterns

by Christopher Gaffney, Vince Gaffney and Martin Tingle

All too often archaeologists have regarded field survey as a source of sites suitable for excavation rather than as a serious analytical tool. The growth of a more rigorous approach to survey is leading us to an appreciation of the full role of this technique.

Without doubt, the main impetus for such research was the desire to recover settlement patterns rather than settlement systems (Flannery, 1976a). This amounts to little more than the quest for the perfect distribution map on which all contemporary settlements are hoped to be represented. So much past work has been site orientated that such maps have been expected to fulfil an explanatory role. This is an unrealistic expectation since they are presenting a purely static picture of a dynamic and complex system.

Less frequently discussed is the disturbingly tenuous link between actual field survey data and the final form and integration of such maps. Those isolated points termed sites were rarely discrete entities. Often they represented only peaks within what could be a highly variable data set, the majority of which was ignored because it would not fit into those preconceived units. Consequently 'settlement vacuums' appeared in those periods or areas which failed to produce sites in the traditional form.

Most European archaeologists have tried to gloss over these embarassing gaps by emphasising the problems caused by widespread disturbance, destruction, alluviation and sample bias. Few considered the more worrying possibility that our conception of human settlement might be inadequate. However, since the mid 1970's a series of significant ethnographic studies has taken place whose results are highly relevant to field survey. These studies have tended to emphasise the significance of discard patterns to all aspects of a society's subsistence activities and have not been limited to the settlement site (Binford, 1983; Gould, 1980; Yellen, 1977).

Whilst hunter gatherer societies have lent themselves to this approach particularly well, studies of complex sedentary communities have also shown the variety of activities which may occur beyond the confines of the settlement (House, 1977; Murray and Chang, 1981).

The result of this research has been the formulation of survey strategies in which the archaeological record is thought to result from activities occurring throughout a landscape. The resulting discard patterns may reflect the differing nature or intensity of activities. A peak in artefact density may represent a 'settlement', but the converse need not be true. Among the studies resulting from this approach are David Hurst Thomas' surveys in the Reese and Monitor valleys (Thomas, 1975; 1983), Bettinger's (1977) research in Owens Valley and Foley's (1981) Amboseli project in Kenya. The results of Shennan's Hampshire survey (Shennan, 1982) show the benefits to be gained by using an 'off site' approach in this country.

The majority of such projects have been regional in scope and have employed large sampling schemes in order to detect behavioural variation across a number of ecological zones. The success of these schemes is due to their ability to integrate these new concepts with practical survey methods and to their appreciation of the nature of the questions that can be answered at this scale (Gaffney and Tingle, forthcoming b).

Research on smaller geographical scales has been less successful. It is significant that even traditional approaches to micro-regional analysis have rarely been productive. The two principle strategies open to micro-regional study, Parish survey and site catchment analysis (referred to as SCA) both suffer from our failure to come to terms with human behaviour at this level.

Parish surveys have fallen by the wayside primarily because the survey area is defined by modern boundaries and need have no specific relevance to past patterns of behaviour. The Parish survey is little more than a geographically convenient grab sample and carries with it all the limitations of such a strategy.

In the past, SCA has been claimed to have a behavioural basis. The land use hypothesis employed here is simple, concise and, all things being equal, rather attractive. The model pioneered by Vita-Finzi and Higgs (1970) states that because of energy costs the intensity of land use around a central settlement will decrease steadily with distance. This model was perhaps the inevitable result of a methodology based on the site. Equally inevitable was the fact that since field survey was concerned mainly with site location such land use models were untestable.

However, the adoption of an 'off site' methodology does allow us to assess the validity of these models. An interesting example of such work has recently been published by Wilkinson (1982). Here Wilkinson has used an extensive sherd sampling technique to define the extent and nature of manuring scatters, and their association with a number of prehistoric and historic towns in Iran, Oman, and Syria. In two of the case studies the scatters were defined by extensive transect survey and provided data on the extent of the material, whilst information from Tell Sweyhat (Syria) was subjected to regression analysis. These analyses related sherd density and manuring intensity with distance from their assumed point of origin in the towns. He obtained correlation co-efficients of -0.68 and -0.72 respectively for linear and log normal correlations. Wilkinson argues that the results provide evidence for a regular decline in manuring intensity with distance and that this provides empirical evidence for the principles of SCA.

However, the present authors believe that this conclusion needs more discussion because it depends upon a series of unqualified assumptions regarding the unique character of the central site. Moreover, both the sampling scheme and the statistical techniques used on the data are self-fulfilling. Our discussion of these problems is discussed under three broad headings.

1. Settlement, Behaviour and Land Use—a Case for Symbiotic Models

Perhaps the most important assumption in Wilkinson is that there is a direct relationship between the central site and the overall pattern of land use. In Wilkinson's study it is assumed that all 'off site' activity represented by manuring deposits can be explained by reference to the central settlement and that the character of the archaeological data was determined entirely by ease of access from this point. The model takes no account of activities which may be exclusive to areas outside the town or to those which may be focussed on other parts of the site territory. A completely centralised economy is assumed without argument.

> 'Although occasional house plans of Sirafi buildings were evident during the survey, they were too distant (greater than 500 m) from the fields for the scatter to be their immediate refuse. In other places where small structures were adjacent to the fields, these appeared to be too humble to be endowed with such fine utensils ... these sherds must have been derived from the city of Siraff.' (Wilkinson 1982: 326)
> 'There were no nearby building remains from which such a scatter could be derived. Again they appear to be originally derived from the main city on the coast.' (Wilkinson 1982: 327)
> 'At several sites ... artefacts could be seen scattered across fields and were clearly different from the occupation scatters immediately adjacent to buildings.' (Wilkinson 1982: 333)

Wilkinson needed to have archaeologically detectable remains in order to investigate manuring but may be confusing the ultimate source of that material with the areas from which it was being deposited. As he notes, in some societies in the Near East compost is a marketable commodity and may have been moved in a series of stages before its final deposition (Wilkinson 1982: 324–325).

Wilkinson's attempted restatement of SCA must be reviewed by again looking at the relationship between human settlement activity and resources. It has been said that the problems with this technique 'only increase when one leaves palaeolithic camps and early Neolithic villages' (Flannery, 1976a: 92). This is certainly true, yet even apparently simple economies may raise problems for SCA. The camps of foraging communities operating with an expedient economy may be located for a whole variety of reasons. Moreover, the activities carried out from such camps may reflect the extremely uneven distribution of resources and defy the strict application of this method.

This problem increases again when communities are logistically organised (Binford, 1983). The importance of this type of pattern among hunter gatherer communities has been highlighted by Binford's work among the Nunamiut Eskimos (Binford, 1979; 1980; 1982; 1983). He has shown how the maintenance of semi-permanent camps may depend on a number of basic choices. These include the separation of activity groups from the main band in order to exploit distant but critical resources. Obviously these camps may be regarded as separate sites, but even so they cannot be studied independently of the community's economy as a whole. The location of the central site may take the position of such camps into account. Such economies demand a degree of integration which is not encompassed by SCA.

The idea of the logistically planned economy has received little attention from those archaeologists studying more complex societies. Kent Flannery's (1976b) work on semi-sedentary farming communities in the Tehuacan valley, Mexico, provides a relevant exception. Flannery notes that during the Middle Formative period, the village of Las Canaos may have maintained temporary camps including the Coxcatlan cave, at some distance from the permanent village.

These temporary sites which were nearly 20 km. away from the central settlement, allowed the repeated seasonal use of resources not directly available to the villagers. Access to these resources was important to the continued success of the settlement. Obviously, we need to understand the whole range of variation present in such an economy. Once again we must conclude that SCA does not take into account the full complexity of human behaviour and for this reason cannot always identify the critical variables within particular economies.

Even complex sedentary societies can practise economies with a logistical basis. Elite groups within ranked societies may use their powers to organise production logistically in order to maintain or even expand their own position. If we ignore the complications created by the development of a market we can still recognise changing patterns in the archaeological record caused by intensification of production at a single site.

In order to do this we must envisage a central point set within an ideal landscape (see Fig. 8.1). All resources are evenly distributed with no physical barriers to access. Utilisation of those resources would depend on their distance from the central point. One would predict a falling intensity of land use with distance as in the

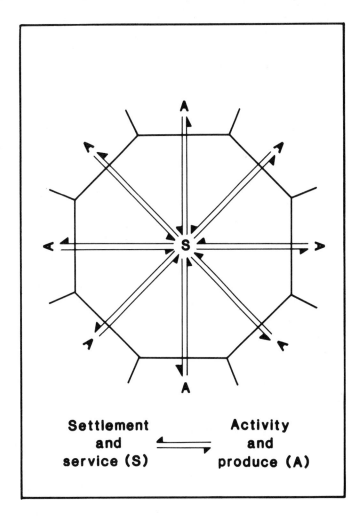

Figure 8.1   Idealised land use model.

traditional Site Catchment model. But if demand increased how would the system react? Land use could be intensified only up to the limits prescribed by that society's technology. If this was insufficient the community might be forced to exploit a larger area of land. In order to do this the energy costs of expansion must be overcome. Since the cost of maintaining the desired level of service activities would increase with distance, it would be necessary to feed off some of these activities into peripheral parts of the intensively utilised area.

The creation of these secondary activity foci would increase the area available for intensive land use. Such foci would still be linked to the central settlement by those services which were not available elsewhere, perhaps food storage or processing facilities. In an ideal landscape it would be most efficient to space these activity areas at fairly regular intervals. The physical remains associated with such activity areas might appear as ephemeral peaks in the survey record and need not be identified intuitively as 'settlement sites'.

This process would extend the amount of land that could be used efficiently from the central settlement. Although it might be argued that the activity areas should be treated as separate sites, the primary and secondary sites are actually interdependent and the overall economy can only be understood in this context. The maintenance and scale of the primary site would be dependant upon the success of the secondary activity areas. Yet traditional SCA would concentrate entirely on the role of the central site. Unless we consider the field evidence for such features as sheep folds, hay ricks, tool sheds and manure heaps, we reduce our chances of understanding early land use.

The full implications of this position can be seen from work carried out by the Maddle Farm Project on the Berkshire Downs. The Maddle Farm Project was initiated to investigate a small Romano-British villa/settlement complex near Upper Lambourn in Berkshire. Excavation carried out on the villa and its settlement has been complemented by extensive field survey.

The survey was carried out in stages (see Fig. 8.2). In the first stage, all the available land within a 2 km. radius circle centred on the villa was walked—a total of 8 km.^{2} of available arable fields. In the second stage this was followed by a larger sampling scheme. This was designed to look at the dominant topography of the chalk downs, and was composed of a series of systematic transects 500 m. wide laid out on an east/west alignment at 500 m. intervals.

Collection occurred within the Ordnance Survey hectare grid located from 1:2500 maps. Within each hectare four 100 m. runs took place at 25 m. intervals, always aligned north-south. Each run was subdivided into two 50 m. traverses, giving a total of eight separate contexts within each hectare. This technique, first developed by Peter Woodward (1978), has certain advantages. Not only are the results standard, but the grid is permanent and nationwide. These features allow direct comparison between surveys using the same method.

Total collection was carried out over selected sites prior to excavation; again, collection took place within the National Grid. The 5 metre collection units were also taken as the framework for subsequent excavation. This has allowed the authors to relate surface and excavated data in order to test total collection results.

Extensive fieldwalking results both on and off site have also been tested by carrying out a limited sub-surface survey. A series of standard quadrats placed at 25 m. intervals along fieldwalking 'runs' were sieved to the natural chalk and the results from the quadrats and survey data were compared. These results indicated that there was a positive relationship between extensive fieldwalking results and the total artefact content of the plough-soil.

The information discussed in this paper refers to the first season's work, when all the available land within a 2 km. radius circle of the villa was walked. Figure 8.3 portrays the distribution of Roman pottery located by survey. Perhaps the most significant point is the fact that only a small proportion of the ceramics were actually restricted to the principal sites—the villa and the settlement. The objects are dispersed over an area of more than 500 hectares. The pottery distribution is highly variable. This variation is not the result of alluviation or other post-depositional processes, nor can the pattern be explained by settlement drift. The principal period of discard was restricted to a few centuries in which there was a demonstrable, permanent centre of settlement, attested through excavation, at the Villa complex. Occupation at this site spanned the immediate post conquest period through to the last decades of the fourth century and perhaps continued into the sub-Roman period.

The most likely explanation for the existence of such quantities of pottery over so large an area is that it represents evidence for the manuring of farmland. Pottery may enter the survey record in this fashion when manure collected at a settlement is mixed with domestic refuse. The manure is then spread on the land in order to maintain its fertility.

On analogy with historically attested farming practises carried out on the Berkshire Downs, the deposition of manure carries a number of implications. During the post medieval period, we know a relatively intensive arable economy could be maintained without large scale manuring. The judicious use of sheep flocks folded on stubble was enough to ensure arable production. Manure from settlements tended to be restricted to areas with winter fodder crops. This economy finds its expression in Figure 8.4 where there is a notable lack of evidence for settlement derived manure. The major exception occurs around the village of Upper Lambourn where the inhabitants who did not have access to large flocks of sheep may have used waste from the settlement areas on

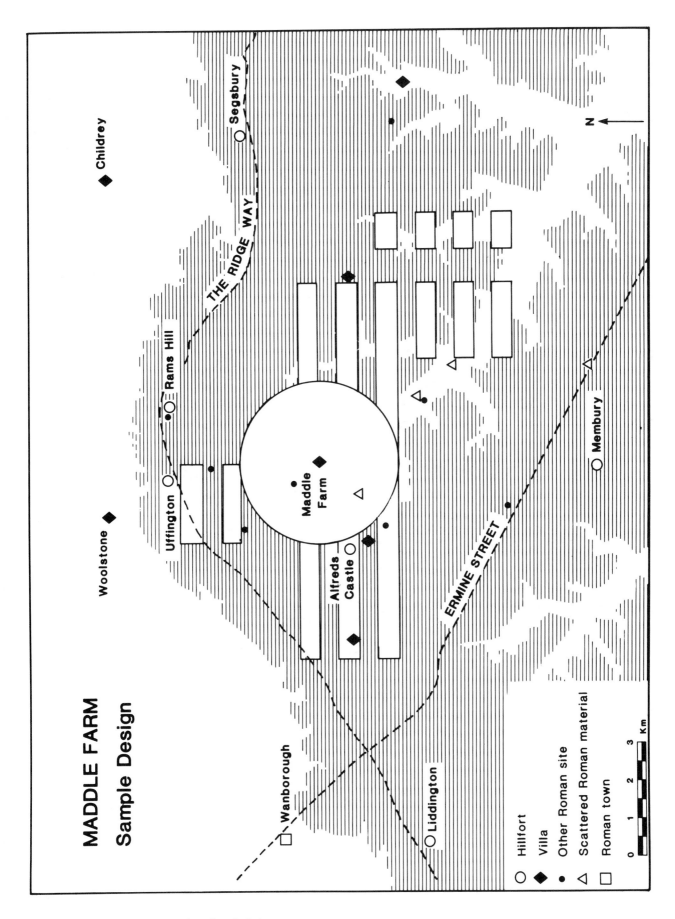

Figure 8.2   The Maddle Farm project: Sample design.

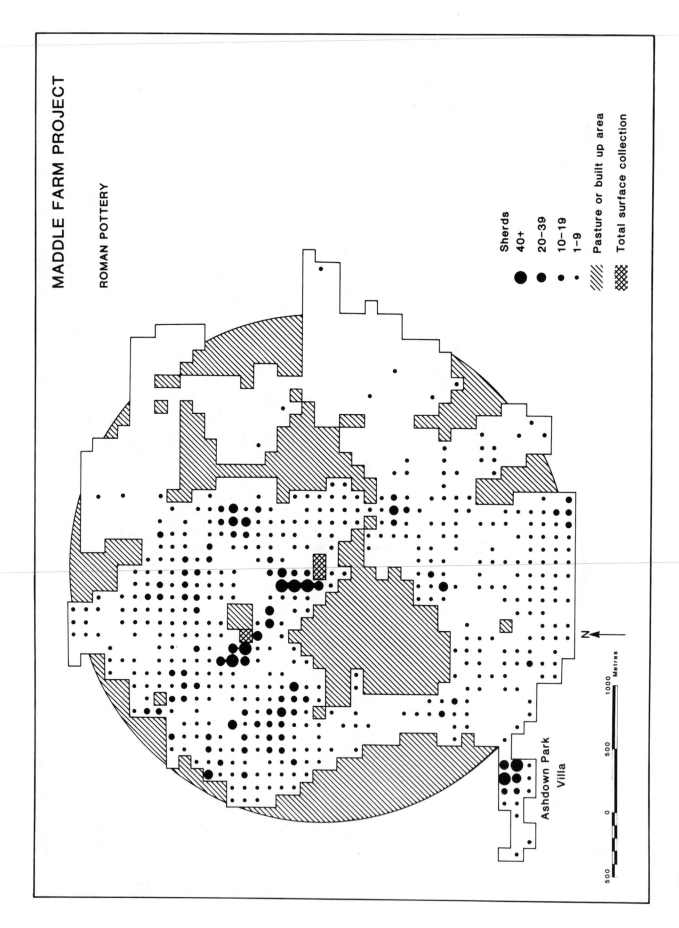

Figure 8.3   Maddle Farm: Roman pottery distribution.

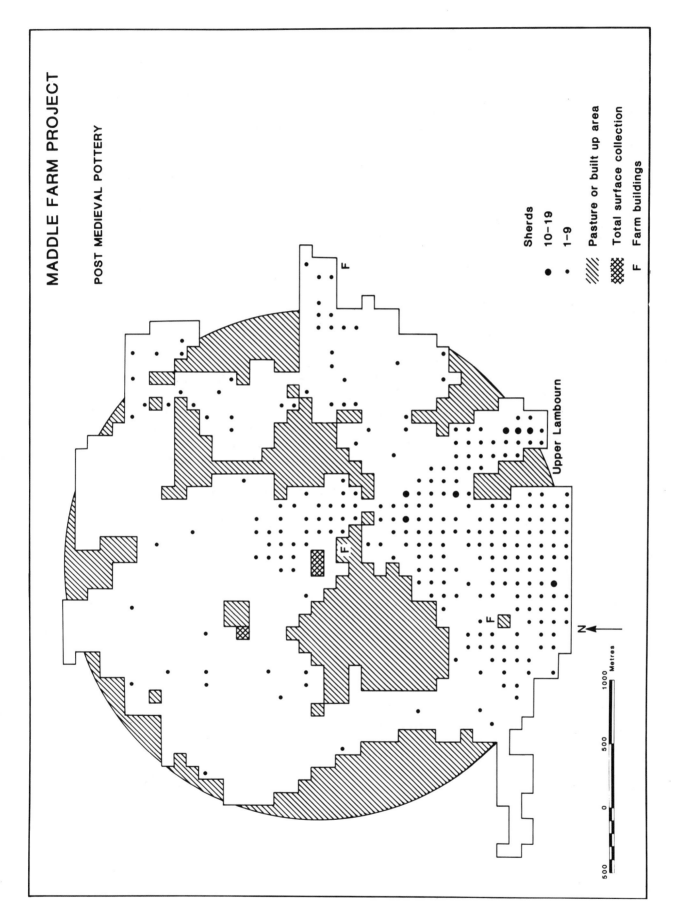

Figure 8.4 Maddle Farm: Post-medieval pottery distribution.

their fields. At this time the arable area extended in long strips across the chalkland and down into the Vale of the White Horse, itself a pattern which could not be recovered by SCA. The economy was maintained by shepherds who lived in caravans away from the village, and who travelled up to twelve miles a day with their flocks.

The greater commitment to manuring during the Roman period provides a significant contrast. The scale and intensity of discard seems to indicate that soils were being depleted probably by intensive cereal production. The demands of arable farming may have necessitated the use of relatively arduous methods of manuring. It seems that the economy was logistically organised. The nature of this arrangement becomes apparent when one considers the variation displayed by the manuring data. The trends contained within this variation are displayed in Figure 8.5. It is apparent that the pottery scatter does not show the simple linear fall off predicted by SCA. The latter method would suggest that the land nearest to the settlement would be the most heavily used. This is not found. The trend diagram shows the area around the settlement is an area of generally high discard. However, within this zone are a series of lower density scatters (Fig. 8.5A). Beyond the zone which saw the most intensive manuring there are found fewer sherds but set at regular intervals within this other area are a series of minor pottery concentrations (Fig. 8.5B).

To interpret these patterns a number of points are worth considering. Manuring presents problems of organisation. It is unlikely that human by-products could supply working requirements. Sheep folding could have been practised, but even if it had been used it cannot have been capable of fulfilling all requirements—otherwise pottery scatters would not occur. It is more likely that herd animals which returned regularly to the settlement would have fulfilled the main needs. For instance, a herd of dairy cattle could have been placed on temporary or permanent pasture close to the settlement in order to facilitate access for milking. Because they were folded so near to the settlement, their manure could be mixed with domestic refuse and then taken to the chosen areas. Pasture associated with such a herd would not need manuring itself and this could well account for the areas without many sherds close to the settlement.

This interpretation would imply quite intensive land use, and it is tempting to link the discovery of the smaller pottery scatters to the same process. We have argued that the costs of manuring arable land a distance from the settlement could have been reduced by ceding activities to the outer zones of the 'site territory'. This would extend the area of efficiently used land. The smaller pottery scatters could be representative of such a process.

Whilst these scatters might represent domestic sites, there is no specific need to relate them to habitation, since they need only be points from which activities were carried out seasonally—hayricks or manure heaps. But whether tool sheds or tied cottages, their even spacing seems to indicate they formed part of a much wider economic organisation geared to a relatively high level of production.

Associated with this evidence of intensive manuring we find the construction of a prestige villa building. It will be important to investigate the relationship between the growth of this site and the whole process of agricultural change.

Thus this evidence hints of the growth of a logistically organised economy, linked to the existence of elite groups capable of organising production to their own ends. These are factors which cannot be recovered through the use of SCA. Again, we must stress the distance dependent model postulated by SCA is valid but only if it is seen in a very much broader context. It is this broader context which is missing in Wilkinson's paper.

2. Human Behaviour and Archaeological Sampling

In another article the authors (Gaffney and Tingle, forthcoming b) have argued that the geographical scale at which archaeologists work has wider implications than simple sample design. Larger scales demand the use of suitable sampling strategies, but the use of such schemes carries an inherent behavioural bias for most archaeological periods. These large surveys are unlikely to provide detailed information on subsistence strategies linked to a specific site. In producing regional data the archaeologist is choosing to provide one set of behavioural patterns—the regional at the cost of those present at micro-regional or macro-regional scales.

Similarly extensive sampling strategies at the micro-regional level such as those carried out by Wilkinson are not able to provide information of the sort produced by the Maddle Farm Project. Their extensive nature makes it likely that they will miss many of the significant anomalies discussed here, for the samples are not designed to detect them. However, the very small sample fraction will provide information on those gross behavioural parameters within which significant activity will occur—in this case the extreme measure of distance dependent manuring. It will not detect the anomalies which condition the shape of such a fall off

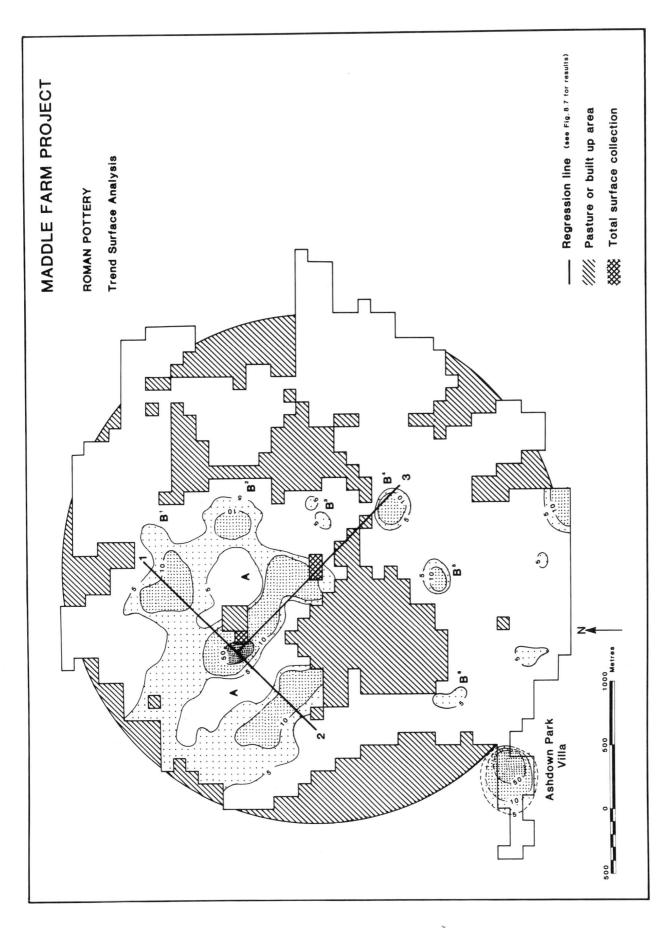

Figure 8.5   Maddle Farm: Trend surface analysis of Roman pottery distribution.

curve. Wilkinson not only accepted a model which assumes that such anomalies cannot exist, but based the hypothesis on a sampling technique which is incapable of showing whether such variations were present in the data. Moreover, the statistics that Wilkinson employs are themselves open to question.

3. The Nature of Regression Analysis

At its simplest, regression analysis is a method of placing the best fit line through a set of data. The correlation coefficient expresses how much of the variation within the data is expressed by that line. Despite the manner in which archaeologists present such analyses, the production of a 'good fit' does not necessarily ascribe complete validity to a given set of assumptions: the correlation coefficient does not ascribe *archaeological* significance to anomalies within the data.

Anscombe (1973) has demonstrated this problem by modelling a series of regressions from widely varying data sets, all of which could vary significantly in their origin. However, all the sets provided the same regression lines and correlation coefficients. The production of a high correlation coefficient is not necessarily significant in itself and, used uncritically, could mask archaeologically significant variation. Another basic problem is that the simple regression so often used in archaeology may assume the importance of only two variables. In considering regression problems with greater numbers of variables (as is usual in most social sciences) 'the likelihood that we fool ourselves by carrying out some ordinary regression calculations is much greater too' (Anscombe, 1973: 21).

In Figure 8.6 we have attempted to illuminate the problem by subjecting a series of ideal data sets to regression analysis. The high correlation coefficients would seem to be evidence of a good fit. The presence of significant anomalies within the simulated data and recent archaeological applications of these techniques indicates how such results could be used to mask variation—even assuming that the techniques used isolated such variability in the first place. Likewise, Maddle Farm data when sampled by radial transects can also provide positive fits, even if the data includes significant anomalies (see Fig. 8.7). The blind acceptance of such tests ignores the true complexity of human behaviour.

In the case of the Tell Swayhat analysis, Wilkinson's use of regression analysis on data produced by a sampling scheme only designed to pick out gross trends is really a self fulfilling exercise. The results produced cannot be expected to ascribe validity to his conclusions, as the one point we can be sure of is that this technique will either not detect anomalies in the model, or it will mask them in the succeeding analysis.

Conclusions

The relevance of field survey to the analysis of human behaviour patterns has been a significant trend within recent years. Perhaps its most significant contribution is that it has managed to free archaeologists from the site as their analytical universe. This enlarged perspective has helped us to reveal the vast range of human activities which can be recognised at different geographical scales extending from the site, to the region and beyond. Because of the complexity of this data archaeologists have sought to isolate regularities which they assume to be significant. Unfortunately, the temptation to simplify the evidence in order to interpret it has led to the formulation of models which are so simplistic that they rarely represent the true nature of past behaviour and limit their own explanatory power.

We believe that SCA and regression analysis in the form presented above are both examples of this trend. We do not doubt that both techniques have something to offer to archaeological analysis. Perhaps the most suitable role for SCA is as an idealised Template against which we may set real data in order to isolate significant variation.

The expansion of the role of analytical field survey has made an already complex archaeological record even more difficult to understand. But in field survey it is this intricacy, and the 'interplay between social distance, subsistence needs and the geometry of location that makes complex settlement systems such an interesting challenge' (Flannery 1976b: 117). If we ignore this challenge it will be at the cost of archaeology's credibility as a discipline.

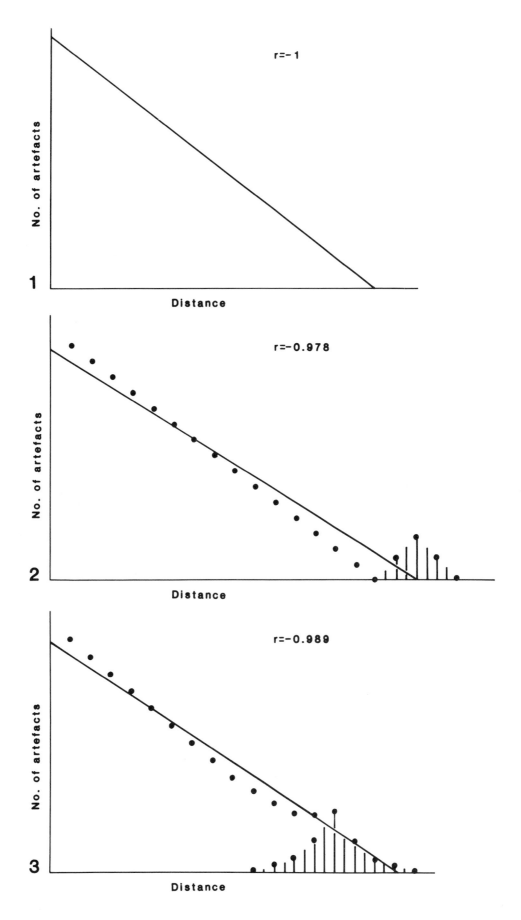

Figure 8.6   Regression analyses using simulated data:
        1.   Perfect fall off.
        2.   Fall off with adjacent archaeologically significant feature.
        3.   Fall off containing archaeologically significant anomaly.

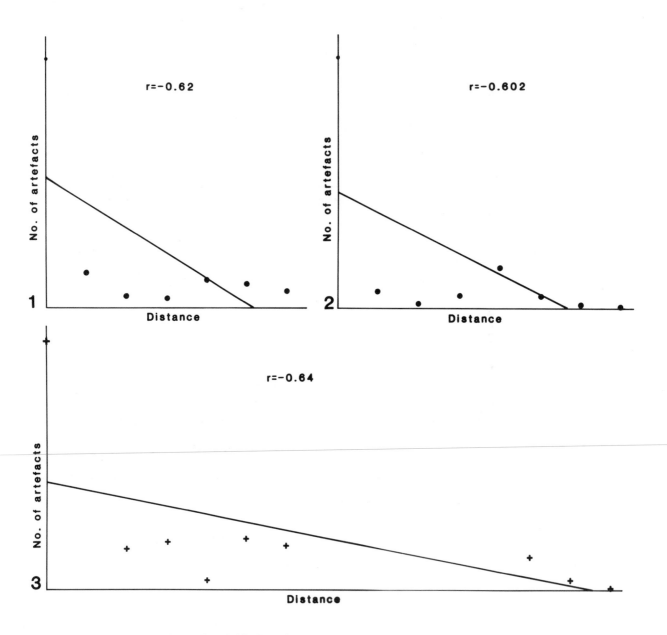

Figure 8.7   Regression analyses using Maddle Farm data:
1. Regression line passing from settlement through low density area and probable activity area.
2. Regression line passing from settlement through low density area (pasture?) into higher sherd discard zone.
3. Regression line from settlement passing through villa and probable activity area.

Acknowledgements

The authors would like to express their appreciation to Richard Bradley for his encouragement, advice and many helpful suggestions. We would also like to thank Jill Mead for typing the manuscript.

Bibliography

Anscombe, F.J. 1973 Graphs in statistical analysis. *The American Statistician* 27: 17–21

Bettinger, R.L. 1977 Aboriginal human ecology in Owens Valley: prehistoric change in the Great Basin. *American Antiquity* 42: 3–17

Binford, L.R. 1979 Organisation and formation processes: looking at curated technologies. *Journal of Anthropological Research* 35: 255–75

Binford, L.R. 1980 Willow smoke and dog's tails: hunter gatherer settlement systems and archaeological site formation. *American Antiquity* 45: 4–20

Binford, L.R. 1982 The archaeology of place. *Journal of Anthropological Archaeology* 1: 5–31

Binford, L.R. 1983 *In Pursuit of the Past: Decoding the Archaeological Record.* London: Thames and Hudson

Flannery, K.V. 1976a Introduction to Chapter 6, Analysis on the regional level, part 1. In *The Early Mesoamerican Village*, K.V. Flannery (ed.) pp. 161–2. London: Academic Press

Flannery, K.V. 1976b Empirical determination of site catchments in Oaxaca and Tehuacan. In *The Early Mesoamerican Village*, K.V. Flannery (ed.) pp. 103–116. London: Academic Press

Foley, R. 1981 *Off site Archaeology and human adaptation in Eastern Kenya Cambridge Monographs in African Archaeology 3.* Oxford: British Archaeological Reports (International series 97)

Gaffney, V. and Tingle, M. Forthcoming a The tyranny of the site. Method and theory in field survey. *Scottish Archaeological Review*

Gaffney, V. and Tingle, M. Forthcoming b *Is Big Always Beautiful? The Maddle Farm Project and Micro-regional Analysis* Society of Antiquaries (Monograph on field survey)

Gould, R.M. 1980 *Living Archaeology.* Cambridge: Cambridge University Press

Higgs, E.S. and Vita-Finzi, C. 1972 Prehistoric economies: a territorial approach. In *Papers in Economic Prehistory*. E.S. Higgs (ed.) pp. 27–36. Cambridge: Cambridge University Press

House, J.H. 1977 Survey data and regional models in historical archaeology. In *Research Strategies in Historical Archaeology*, S. South (ed.) pp. 241–60 London: Academic Press

Murray, P. and Chang, C. 1981 An ethnoarchaeological study of a contemporary herder's site *Journal of Field Archaeology* 8: 372–88

Shennan, S.J. 1982 Settlement history in East Hampshire. In *The Archaeology of Hampshire from the Palaeolithic to the Industrial Revolution*. R.T. Schadla-Hall and S.J. Shenhan (eds.) pp. 106–21 Hampshire Field Club and Archaeological Society Monograph No. 1

Thomas, D.H. 1975 Non site sampling in archaeology: up the creek without a site. In *Sampling in Archaeology* J.W. Mueller (ed.) pp. 61–81 Tucson: University of Arizona Press

Thomas, D.H. 1983 The archaeology of Monitor Valley: 1 epistemology *Anthropological Papers of the American Museum of Natural History* 58

Vita-Finzi, C. and Higgs, E.S. 1970 Prehistoric economy in the Mt. Carmel area of Palestine: site catchment analysis. *Proceedings of the Prehistoric Society* 36: 1–37

Wilkinson, T.J. 1982 The definition of ancient manured zones by means of extensive sherd sampling techniques. *Journal of Field Archaeology* 9: 323–33

Woodward, P. 1978 A problem-orientated approach to the recovery of knapped flint debris: a fieldwalking strategy for answering questions posed by the site distributions and excavations. In *Sampling in Contemporary British Archaeology*. J.F. Cherry, C. Gamble and S. Shennan (eds.) pp. 121–128. Oxford: British Archaeological Reports British Series 50

Yellen, J.E. 1977 *Archaeological Approaches to the Present.* London: Academic Press

Summaries—Zusammenfassungen—Resumées

1. Inference from ploughsoil artefact samples
C.C. Haselgrove

Although the systematic collection of artefacts from cultivated land in surveys conducted at both local and regional scales plays an important role in contemporary archaeology, there has been relatively little discussion of how one can make the best use of the "window on the past" which the destructive agency of ploughing affords us, or what sort of questions about settlement patterns field survey can hope to answer. Using examples drawn mainly from Iron Age and Roman contexts, this paper considers, *(1)* the need to construct a methodology specific to the evaluation of ploughsoil finds, *(2)* the factors which must be taken into account and the underlying assumptions which are generally made in the interpretation of such material, and *(3)* how some of the main problems of field survey data may be either controlled or circumvented.

1. Auswertung von Pflugboden-Funden
C.C. Haselgrove

Die Ansammlung der Streufunde aus kultiviertem Boden in Untersuchungen auf lokaler und regionaler Ebene spielt eine wichtige Rolle in der zeitgenössischen Archäologie; immerhin wird verhältnismässig wenig darüber ausgesagt, wie man guten Gebrauch machen kann von jenem "Fenster zur Vergangenheit", und was für Fragen über Ansiedlungstendenzen beantwortet werden können. Die Studie zieht hauptsächlich Beispiele aus der Eisen- und Römerzeit heran und diskutiert: *(1)* die Notwendigkeit eine Methodologie einzuführen, die besonders für die Auswertung der Versammlungen entwickelt worden ist; *(2)* die Faktoren die man erwägen und die unterliegenden Voraussetzungen, die man anerkennen muss; und *(3)* wie man einige der Hauptprobleme der Feldstudien-Daten entweder kontrolliert oder umgangen werden könnten.

1. Qu'est-ce qu'on peut déduire à partir de ramassages de surface?
C.C. Haselgrove

Le rôle de programmes de prospections de surface systématiques, conduites à l'échelle locale et régionale, est d'une importance essentielle dans l'archéologie d'aujourd'hui. Le labour, tout en détruisant des sites archéologiques, nous offre des «fenêtres sur le passé». Cependant, on ne discute ni le moyen de tirer de meilleurs informations de ces «fenêtres», ni les questions de la répartition de structures d'habitat, dont les solutions pourrait être livrées par la prospection au sol. Cette étude se sert d'exemples tirés pour la plupart de contextes de l'Age du Fer et de l'époque romaine afin d'examiner: *(1)* la nécessité de développer une méthodologie spécifique à l'évaluation de ramassages de surface; *(2)* les facteurs pertinents à une telle methodologie, ainsi que les suppositions que l'on fait dans l'interpretation de trouvailles; et *(3)* les moyennes de controller ou éviter quelques-uns des problèmes que posent les données recueillies lors de prospections au sol.

2. Field survey calibration: a contribution
M. Millett

This paper approaches the problem of variation in the amount of archaeological material which archaeologists record in different periods. It uses quantified data from two recent excavations to show their potential for calibrating the results of field survey work. The importance of collecting further information about the quantities of material present on excavations cannot be over-stressed.

2. Landesaufnahmevermessung: ein Beitrag
M. Millett

Die folgende Darstellung befasst sich mit den unterschiedlichen Mengen des archäologischen Materials, die in verschiedenen Zeitaltern gefunden werden. Quantifiziertes Material von zwei neuen Ausgrabungen wird als Beispiel untersucht, um das Potential der Messung der Landuntersuchungergebnisse darzustellen. Die Wichtigkeit der zukünftigen Forschung über die quantifizierte Menge der Grabungsfunde kann nicht genug betont werden.

2. «Calibrage» dans la prospection de surface
M. Millett

Cette étude aborde le problème de variation dans la quantité de vestiges archéologiques de toutes les époques que repèrent les archéologues. On se sert de renseignements de deux fouilles, de façon à en démontrer la potentialité pour le «calibrage» de résultats de programmes de prospection de surface. On met l'accent sur la nécessité de recueillir des renseignements de plus en ce qui concerne les quantités d'objets fouillés, afin de vérifier en stratigraphie les éléments statistiques repérés au sol.

3. Sample bias, regional analysis and fieldwalking in British archaeology
N. Mills

The primary objectives of this paper are to examine the limitations of our present knowledge of the distribution of all types of archaeological evidence. It suggests that our knowledge can be improved by a sequence of new studies of different regions which pay particular attention to local variations in distribution patterns. Such surveys would provide reliable samples of the evidence to serve planning, education and research. The skills needed for such survey, and the present lack of training programmes are stressed. It is suggested that such training should include an appreciation of landscape change/geomorphology; the processes leading to the deposition of artefacts; and those affecting them after deposition; together with a full knowledge of fieldwalking techniques and sampling theory.

The paper finally analyses the limitations of our present British data in relation to differences both in preservation and in methods of data collection and recording. These problems are discussed in relation to early agricultural communities, and a series of suggestions are made about how information can be improved.

3. Probeneigung, regionale Landesaufnahme und Geländebegehung
N. Mills

Das Hauptziel dieses Papiers ist die Begrenzung unserer heutigen Kenntnis über die Verbreitung archäologischen Materiales darzustellen. Diese Lage kann, durch neue Untersuchungen von verschiedenen Regionen und insbesondere lokalisierte Verbreitungstendenzen, verbessert werden. Eine solche Strategie würde zu verlässlichen Beweisen für zukünftige Planung, Ausbildung und Forschung führen. Die nötige Geschicklichkeit für eine solche Landesaufnahme, und den jetzigen Mangel an Ausbildung werden unterstrichen. Man schlägt vor, dass ein solches Training ein Verständnis für Geomorphologie für die Prozesse, die den archäologischen Befund beeinflussen, und die Prozesse danach einschliessen sollte; auch—eine gründliche Kenntnis der Begehungsmethoden und Probetherapien.

Zum Schluss werden die Begrenzungen des heutigen Materials in Grossbritannien, im Zusammenhang mit ihrer unterschiedlichen Erhaltung und der verschiedenen Landesaufnahmemethoden, besprochen. Diese Probleme sind in der Auswertung neolithischer Siedlungen gut zu sehen; und der Autor schlägt vor, wie man diese Lage verbessern kann.

3. Prospection de surface, analyse régionale, et problèmes d'échantillonnage dans l'archéologie en Grande-Bretagne
N. Mills

L'objet principale de cette étude est l'examination des limitations de notre connaissance de la distribution de vestiges archéologiques. On suggère qu'il faut des programmes de prospection de surface, dans des régions diverses, qui ont égard aux variations locales dans la répartition du mobilier en surface. Il faut aussi de l'habilité pour faire une telle prospection, mais il y a un manque de programmes de formation. Un programme de formation doit tenir compte de géomorphologie; du processus de la déposition, de la préservation, ainsi que de la modification d'artefacts; en même temps que des techniques de prospection de surface et des théories d'échantillonnage.

Cette étude conclut par analyser les limitations des données actuelles en G.–B. par rapport aux différences de préservation et de différences dans les méthodes de les recueillir et les noter. L'exemple proposé est celui de communautés agriculturelles anciennes, et on suggère comment on pouvait perfectionner nos renseignements.

4. Identifying neolithic settlements in Britain: the role of field survey in the interpretation of lithic scatters
R. Holgate

Many kinds of sites are relatively impervious to discovery through methods other than field survey, e.g. Neolithic domestic sites in Britain. For them, lithic artefact scatters often provide the only obvious pointer. The aim of the paper is to present a surface collection survey design which could be used to define likely areas of domestic activity. Within a near-continuous distribution of artefacts across the landscape, concentrations of lithic material are to be expected; the problem is how to interpret them? Many variables can bring about their formation, among them post-depositional transport, biases arising out of collection procedures and even differences in the availability of the original raw materials. However, provided these factors can be identified, it should be possible to isolate those remaining concentrations which represent the loci of past human activity. The approach is assessed in terms of the results of a survey in the Abingdon area of the Upper Thames Valley. As far as Neolithic domestic sites are concerned, field survey can only put dots on the map for the present—itself of value given the abysmal state of current knowledge. Once the controls afforded by planned excavations can be deployed, it should be possible to go further and determine the activities practised at particular locations from surface remains alone.

4. Die Rolle der Landesaufnahme in der Auswertung der Verbreitung von Streusteinfunden
R. Holgate

Viele verschiedene archäologische Fundstätte sind nur durch Landesaufnahme identifiziert worden, z.B. neolithische Siedlungen in Grossbritannien. In diesem Fall sind Streusteinfunde der einzig gute Beweis dafür. Das folgende Papier möchte versuchen eine Geländebegehungsstrategie darzustellen, die mögliche Siedlungs- oder Aktivitätszonen andeuten kann. Innerhalb einer fast ununterbrochenen Verbreitung der Streufunde, wird man Konzentrationen von Material finden. Aber ihre Auswertung ist immernoch sehr problematisch. Viele verschiedene Faktoren sind verantwortlich dafür, z.B. geomorphologische Prozesse, Probleme der Geländebegehungsmethoden, und die unterschiedliche Verfügbarkeit des Rohmaterials. Aber wenn diese Faktoren identifiziert worden sind, wird die Möglichkeit bestehen, die übrige Konzentrationen zu erkennen, die diese Aktivitätszonen vertreten müssen. Die Ergebnisse einer Landesaufnahme aus der Abingdon Umgebung der Upper Thames Valley wird hier besprochen. In Bezug auf neolithische Siedlungen, jedoch, bleibt die Landesaufnahme als Forschungsmethode ziemlich unergiebig, aber immerhin enorm wertvoll, wenn wir den heutigen Kenntnisstand betrachten. Wenn die Kontrollen der geplanten Ausgrabungen verwendet werden können, muss die Möglichkeit bestehen, Fortschritte zu machen, und diese Siedlungsaktivitäten nur von Streufunden zu erkennen.

4. La reconnaissance d'habitats néolithiques en Grande-Bretagne: le rôle de prospection au sol dans l'interprétation de ramassages de surface lithiques
R. Holgate

On ne trouve plusieurs types de sites (d'habitats néolithiques en G.–B., par exemple) que par la prospection de surface. Souvent les seuls témoins sont les trouvailles lithiques au sol. Il faut une méthode de prospection de surface qui pourrait aider à définir des zones d'activités. Entre des aires avec trouvailles de surface éparsés on s'attend des concentrations d'artefacts: mais comment les interpreter? Il se peut qu'il s'agisse de déplacement après l'enfouissement; de différentes méthodes de prospection; on bien de différences dans la disponibilité de matière première. Cependant, pourvu qu'on puisse identifier ces variables, on devrait pouvoir isoler les concentrations qui représentent des sites véritables. Quant aux sites néolithiques, la prospection de surface ne peut nous donner que des cartes de répartition de sites—de valeur, étant donné notre ignorance fondamentale. Le deuxième étape sera fouiller quelques-uns des sites repérés. Ainsi pourrait-on déterminer les activités pratiqués à certains sites à partir de vestiges en surface. L'example proposé est celui d'une prospection au sol autour d'Abingdon, Upper Thames Valley.

5. Approaching The Fens the fexible way
D. Crowther, C. French and F. Pryor

Recent work on the prehistory of the Fens is used to illustrate the potential of an opportunistic approach to the survey of a wet environment. A variety of environmental and archaeological approaches are examined, the potential of wet and dry sites is compared, and the processes which alter the archaeological record after burial are fully assessed. The conclusion that wet areas offer an enormous potential is drawn, and the problems of examining such a deeply buried landscape are investigated. Finally, the practical approach to examining these buried landscapes, through the investigation of exposures in dykes, is discussed.

5. Untersuchung der Sumpflandschaften (The Fens) auf bewegliche Weise
D. Crowther, C. French und F. Pryor

Neue Forschung über die Vorgeschichte der Sumpflandschaften wird als Beispiel dargestellt, um den Wert einer rechtzeitigen Landesaufnahme in solchen fortlaufenden, nassen Umgebungen zu zeigen. Verschiedene Umwelt- und archäologische Methoden werden untersucht, das Potential der trockenen und nassen Fundplätze wird verglichen, und die Prozesse, die den archäologischen Befund beeinflussen, werden gründlich besprochen. Der Beschluss ist, dass eine fortlaufende nasse Umgebung enorm aufschlussreich sei, und die Probleme einer tiefen Altlandschaft werden untersucht. Zum Schluss, werden die praktische Methoden der Altlandschaftsaufnahme, durch die Untersuchung von Deichstrukturen, dargestellt.

5. Une approche flexible pour les marais (The Fens)
D. Crowther, C. French et F. Pryor

Des études récentes de la préhistoire des marais servent à illustrer la potentialité d'une approche «opportuniste» à la prospection d'une environnement humide. On examine quelques approches archéologiques ainsi qu'écologiques; on fait la comparaison des possibilitiés entre les sites humides et les sites secs; et le processus de préservation et de déstruction est évalué. Notre conclusion sera que ce sont les zones humides qui nous offrent le plus, donc sont examinées les problèmes rencontrées lors de la recherche d'un tel paysage profondément enterré. Enfin, on discute l'approche pratique pour l'étude de ces paysages: c'est-à-dire l'inspection attentive des fossés de drainage.

6. "One cannot dig at random in a Peat Bog"
E. Cloutman and R.T. Schadla-Hall

The authors review the development of their strategy for investigating an early Postglacial buried landscape in the Vale of Pickering. They present the results of a sub-surface palaeoenvironmental survey of a site at Seamer Carr, undertaken in an attempt to locate sites comparable to that previously excavated at Star Carr. The paper explains the evolution of their strategy, and stresses the scale of the practical problems involved in investigating such a large area of wet, buried landscape. It concludes that a regional approach based on palaeoenvironmental survey is essential.

6. "Man kann nicht willkürlich im Torfmoor graben"
E. Cloutman und R.T. Schadla-Hall

Die Autoren besprechen die Entwicklung einer Untersuchungsstrategie für eine nacheiszeitliche Altlandschaft im Vale of Pickering. Die Ergebnisse einer unterirdischen Aufnahme der Paläoumgebung von Seamer Carr werden dargestellt, um vergleichbare Fundplätze zu den schon ausgegrabenen Star Carr festzustellen. Die Autoren erklären wie sie ihre Strategie entwickelt haben, und betonen die enormen praktischen Probleme, die bei Untersuchung einer grossen, nassen Altlandschaft, in Betracht gezogen werden müssen. Die Notwendigkeit einer regionalen Aufnahme der Paläoumgebung wird behauptet.

6. «On ne peut pas fouiller au hasard une tourbière»
E. Cloutman et R.T. Schadla-Hall

Les auteurs développent une stratégie de recherche pour un paysage caché qui date au début de l'époque postglaciaire. Ils donnent les résultats d'une étude paléoécologique du sous-sol au site de Seamer Carr. L'objet de cette recherche est de trouver des sites semblables à celui de Star Carr, fouillé antérieurement. Les auteurs montrent l'évolution de leur stratégie. La recherche d'une zone humide avec des paysages anciens cachés pose des problèmes pratiques. On met l'accent sur l'échelle de celles ci. Il faut une approche régionale fondée sur des recherches paléoécologiques.

7. Survey of a settlement: a strategy for the Etruscan site at Doganella in the Albegna Valley, South West Tuscany
L. Walker

Three of the main problems of 'on site' survey are discussed. Such survey provides an approach bridging the gap between regional survey and excavation, where new methods are being developed. It examines how these problems can be resolved, and illustrates this with an Etruscan example from Italy. The author stresses the need for the development of three sets of models, to explain the meaning of ploughsoil finds, to record and retrieve them, and to interpret surface scatters. These models must take into account both the processes involved which determine what will be left for the archaeologists and what will be altered before discovery.

Finally, the interdependence of survey and excavation is stressed, and attention is drawn to the necessity of the latter for providing chronologies for artefacts recovered from the surface.

7. Die Untersuchung einer Fundstelle: Eine Strategie für die etruskische Fundstelle in Doganella im Albegna Tal, der Südwest-toskana
L. Walker

Drei Probleme der Untersuchung eines grossen archäologischen Fundplatzes werden dargestellt. Regionale Landesaufnahme—und Ausgrabungsmethoden die heute immer noch nicht völlig entwickelt worden sind, werden zusammengezogen. Ein etruskisches Beispiel aus Italien erläutet wie man diese Probleme bewältigen kann. Die Autorin betont die Entwicklung dreier Modelle, um die Bedeutung deren Streufunde, Geländebegehungsmethoden, und Auswertung zu erklären. Diese Modelle müssen die Prozesse, die die Entstehung des archäologischen Befundes beeinflusst haben, und deren Folgen, in Betracht ziehen. Zum Schluss wird die gegenseitige Abhängigkeit der Landesaufnahme und Ausgrabung, und die Wichtigkeit der Grabungsstrategie für die chronologische Auswertung der verbundenen Streufunden, betont.

7. Prospection d'un habitat: stratégie de prospection au sol pour la site étrusque à Doganella dans la vallée d'Albegna, S.W. Toscane
L. Walker

L'étude détaillée de la répartition des vestiges sur des sites déjà repérés («on-site survey») comble une lacune entre les prospections régionales et la fouille. Il y a quand même quelques problèmes la-dessus dont trois sont en discussion ici. L'exámple d'un site étrusque démontre un moyen d'éclaircir ces problèmes. Il faut trois séries de modèles: *(1)* afin d'expliquer ce que signifient les trouvailles; *(2)* afin de savoir les noter et les recueillir; *(3)* ainsi que savoir interpreter les ramassages de surface. Les modèles doivent tenir compte des raisons pour la conservation, la modification, ou la destruction de vestiges archéologiques. Enfin, on souligne le fait que la prospection de surface et la fouille s'enchaine, tous deux dépendent l'une de l'autre, et qu'il faut cette dernière afin de fournir des indications plus précises sur la chronologie des trouvailles livrées par la première.

8. Settlement, economy and behaviour
C. Gaffney, V. Gaffney and M. Tingle

The application of the "off-site" approach to survey is investigated in the context of detailed survey of a Romano-British landscape in Berkshire. The authors criticise previous approaches to the reconstruction of behaviour patterns through survey, and in particular demonstrate the limitations of methods like Site Catchment Analysis which over-simplify the data. The off-site data from Berkshire are used to reconstruct the activities associated with a Roman villa, and to show the potential of this method. Stress is laid on the complexity of the data from detailed field survey which, nevertheless, yields information of very considerable potential.

8. Ansiedlung—Landwirtschaft—Verhaltensweise
C. Gaffney, V. Gaffney und M. Tingle

Aufnahme der landwirtschaftlichen Umgebung eines archäologischen Fundplatzes wird untersucht—in diesem Fall die Landesaufnahme einer römischen Landschaft in Berkshire. Die Autoren beurteilen frühere Auswertungen der Aktivitätszonen von Landesaufnahmergebnissen; und insbesondere werden die Probleme der regionalen Naturräumeanalysen dargestellt. Das Beispiel aus Berkshire zeigt wie man die Aktivitätszonen, die mit einer römischen Villa verbunden sind, rekonstruieren kann, und betont das Potential dieser Methode. Besonders unterstrichen wird die Verwickeltheit der Ergebnisse einer intensiven Landesaufnahme. Immerhin sind die Aufschlüsse davon sehr wichtig für zukünftige Forschungen.

8. Habitat, économie et organisation
C. Gaffney, V. Gaffney et M. Tingle

L'étude détaillée d'un paysage Romano-Britannique en Berkshire se sert d'une méthode de prospection de surface dite «hors-de-site» ('off-site survey'). Les auteurs critiquent les modèles interprétatifs traditionnels, et en particulier ils montrent les limitations de méthodes comme «Site-Catchment Analysis» qui simplifient par trop les données. Les données recueillies par la méthode «hors-de-site» en Berkshire servent à déterminer les activités associés à un villa romain, ainsi que démontrer la potentialité de cette méthode. On met l'accent sur la complexité des données livrées par une prospection au surface détaillée. Elles donnent, pourtant, des renseignements importants.

Index